Pacific
Island
Economies

Christopher Browne

D1477369

INTERNATIONAL MONETARY FUND

Production: IMF, Multimedia Services Division, Creative Services
Cover design: Massoud Etemadi
The cover depicts a palm leaf and a map of selected Pacific islands.

Cataloging-in-Publication Data

Browne, Christopher, 1944–

Pacific Island economies / Christopher Browne — [Washington, D.C. : International
Monetary Fund, 2006]
    p. cm.
  ISBN 1-58906-516-6
  1. Islands of the Pacific — Economic policy. 2. Islands of the Pacific — Economic
conditions. 3. Foreign exchange rates — Islands of the Pacific. 4. Emigrant
remittances — Islands of the Pacific. I. International Monetary Fund.

HC681.B76 2006

Price: $25.00

Address orders to:
International Monetary Fund, Publication Services
700 19th Street, N.W., Washington, DC 20431, U.S.A.
Tel.: (202) 623-7430   Telefax: (202) 623-7201
E-mail: publications@imf.org
Internet: http://www.imf.org

recycled paper

Contents

The following conventions are used in this publication:

In tables, a blank cell indicates "not applicable," ellipsis points (. . .) indicate "not available," and 0 or 0.0 indicates "zero" or "negligible." Minor discrepancies between sums of constituent figures and totals are due to rounding.

An en dash (–) between years or months (for example, 2005–06 or January–June) indicates the years or months covered, including the beginning and ending years or months; a slash or virgule (/) between years or months (for example, 2005/06) indicates a fiscal or financial year, as does the abbreviation FY (for example, FY2006).

"Billion" means a thousand million; "trillion" means a thousand billion.

As used in this publication, the term "country" does not in all cases refer to a territorial entity that is a state as understood by international law and practice. As used here, the term also covers some territorial entities that are not states but for which statistical data are maintained on a separate and independent basis.

Foreword

The Pacific island region has considerable potential for development, especially in the areas of tourism, fisheries, forestry, mining, and agriculture. With these resources and the continued substantial economic assistance from donors that is expected, it is certainly feasible to lift these countries' medium-term economic growth record, improve human development indicators, and reduce poverty. Experience since independence demonstrates that the traditional way of life can be preserved, even while the processes of development create modern institutions and help to meet changing aspirations.

The Pacific island countries face many challenges in developing their economies and raising living standards, including their small size, distance from major markets, and vulnerability to natural disasters. Successfully overcoming these challenges will require the continuation of macroeconomic stability and increased emphasis on the structural reforms to which island governments are committed, including improved public sector efficiency and greater private sector activity. While recognizing that important economic, political, and cultural differences exist between the islands, there are a range of policy recommendations that are widely applicable throughout the region.

The International Monetary Fund has for many years enjoyed regular, open, and fruitful discussions on economic policy with all the member countries in the region. This dialogue is now being intensified through more frequent staff visits. The islands have made only limited use of IMF resources in the past, but financial support can always be considered when needed.

The IMF will also continue to play a key role in providing technical assistance to the region, particularly through the Pacific Financial Technical Assistance Center (PFTAC). This institution is located in Suva, Fiji, and serves 15 Pacific island countries: Cook Islands, Federated States of Micronesia, Fiji, Kiribati, Marshall Islands, Nauru, Niue, Palau, Papua New Guinea, Samoa, Solomon Islands, Tokelau, Tonga, Tuvalu, and Vanuatu. It is funded by the Asian Development Bank, Australia, the IMF, Japan, the Republic of Korea, and New Zealand.

This book provides an assessment of regional issues that are currently being addressed by economic policymakers. The country-specific chapters, which comprise the second half of the book, provide in each case a broad overview of the main factors affecting the countries' individual economic performance since independence and the main challenges that lie ahead.

David Burton
Director, Asia and Pacific Department

Acknowledgments

This volume is a collective effort, authored by economists of the IMF's Asia and Pacific Department (APD) who have worked on Pacific Island countries. The project was conducted under the general guidance of Christopher Browne, Assistant Director, APD, who authored several chapters and reviewed the remaining chapters. Steven Dunaway, Deputy Director of APD, provided helpful comments. Fritz R. Pierre-Louis from APD finalized the charts and tables. We are particularly grateful to Linda Griffin Kean of the IMF's External Relations Department, who edited the manuscript and coordinated production of the book.

The views expressed are those of the authors and do not necessarily reflect those of the IMF, its Executive Board, or its management.

Abbreviations

ADB	Asian Development Bank
AML	anti–money laundering
AML/CFT	anti–money laundering and combating the financing of terrorism
BCBS	Basel Committee on Banking Supervision
CARICOM	Caribbean Community and Common Market
CCQG	Council on the Cost and Quality of Government
CET	common external tariff
CFT	combating the financing of terrorism
Compact I	original Compact of Free Association with the United States, 1987–2003 (Marshall Islands, Micronesia, and Palau)
Compact II	renewed Compact of Free Association with the United States, 2004–23 (Marshall Islands, Micronesia, and Palau)
ECCU	Eastern Caribbean Currency Union
ECTEL	Eastern Caribbean Telecommunications Authority
EEZ	exclusive economic zone
EMU	European Monetary Union
EPA	Economic Partnership Agreement (with the European Union)
EU	European Union
FATF	Financial Action Task Force on Money Laundering
FDI	foreign direct investment
FDIC	Federal Deposit Insurance Corporation (United States)
FORSEC	Pacific Islands Forum Secretariat
FSM	Federated States of Micronesia
GDP	gross domestic product
IDA	International Development Association (World Bank)
IMF	International Monetary Fund
MDGs	Millennium Development Goals
PACER	Pacific Agreement on Closer Economic Relations

PIC	Pacific island country
PICTA	Pacific Island Countries Trade Agreement
The Plan	Pacific Plan for Strengthening Regional Cooperation and Integration
PNG	Papua New Guinea
PPAC	Pacific Plan Action Committee
RAMSI	Regional Assistance Mission to the Solomon Islands
RERF	Revenue Equalization Reserve Fund (Kiribati)
RMI	Republic of the Marshall Islands
RTFP	Regional Trade Facilitation Program
SI	Solomon Islands
UN	United Nations
VAGST	value-added tax on goods and services
VAT	value-added tax
WTO	World Trade Organization

I

REGIONAL ISSUES

Overview of Regional Economic Performance and Prospects

Christopher Browne

The island countries of the Pacific region face many challenges in developing their economies and raising living standards over the medium term.[1] Most of these countries enjoyed generally favorable domestic and external conditions at the time of their independence in the 1970s and 1980s, but more recently have faced an increasing number of macroeconomic hurdles. For all countries in the region, these include slower economic growth, increased poverty, heightened governance concerns, lack of private sector activity, limited regional integration (including of labor markets), and questions about aid effectiveness. In several parts of the region, there are additional concerns about a lack of fiscal discipline and potential political uncertainties.

There have been some notable achievements since 2003. Solomon Islands continues to achieve good progress in building on the positive impact of the intervention in 2003 by the Regional Assistance Mission to the Solomon Islands (RAMSI). Papua New Guinea has raised official external reserves to historically high levels through macro stability and higher oil and mineral export prices, and the government appears likely to complete its full term in 2007. Fiji is enjoying strong tourism growth, which helps to offset the loss of textile markets and the potential loss of sugar markets in 2007. Samoa, Tonga, and Vanuatu are receiving more reliable airline service through a partnership with an Australian airline. Marshall Islands and Micronesia are successfully implementing the renewed Compact of Free Association with the United States (Compact II), which runs through 2023.

---

[1]The 10 Pacific island IMF member countries are Fiji, Kiribati, Republic of the Marshall Islands (RMI), Federated States of Micronesia (FSM), Palau, Papua New Guinea (PNG), Samoa, Solomon Islands (SI), Tonga, and Vanuatu.

Perhaps the most positive sign was the final approval by Pacific Forum leaders at their meeting in Papua New Guinea in October 2005 of the Pacific Plan, an ambitious strategy to strengthen regional cooperation and integration over the next 10 years (the Plan is outlined in Chapter 4). It was prepared by the Pacific Islands Forum Secretariat, with the strong endorsement of Australia and New Zealand, and addresses most priority needs, including the need to promote the private sector, strengthen public enterprise reforms, address corruption and law-and-order problems, and encourage integration and trade liberalization. The overall emphasis is on the importance of structural reforms, which is welcome. Of course, the key to the Plan's success will be the pace of its implementation, which depends on the support of Pacific island countries, civil society and private sector organizations, development partners, and other stakeholders for regional approaches to addressing the region's existing capacity constraints and lack of economic opportunities. Regionalism under the Plan does not imply any limitations on national sovereignty. The main objective is to support and complement national programs, not to replace them.

There will be close monitoring and evaluation by the Pacific Islands Forum Secretariat of implementation of the Plan's initiatives. Detailed indicators have been incorporated into the Plan to measure progress during the first three years. The initiatives proposed for this initial period relate to encouraging development of National Sustainable Development Strategies; promoting good governance through transparent, accountable, and equitable management of all resources, assisted by the establishment of anticorruption institutions; strengthening infrastructure, especially in telecommunications and transport; enhancing regional integration in trade and labor markets; and increasing security through safer social and political conditions.

While these initiatives are encouraging, the challenges remain formidable, especially to achieving the goal of faster, sustainable economic development. The region has clearly experienced relatively low growth performance, although it is also evident that inflation has been less serious than in other developing country regions (Table 1.1). Some worrying fiscal deficits have been brought under control, most notably in Papua New Guinea and Solomon Islands, but insufficient public expenditure control, transparency, and accountability remain of concern in many countries. On the external front, the countries of the region have largely avoided balance of payments and debt problems, in part with the help of generous aid receipts. Exchange rate policies have been generally appropriate, with basket pegs or dollarization, except for the floating regime in Papua New Guinea.

Nevertheless, current conditions fall far short of what is needed to secure the medium-term growth objective. In particular, the authorities of

Table 1.1. Selected Indicators for Pacific Island Countries[1]

	1993	1994	1995	1996	1997	1998	1999	2000	2001	2002	2003	2004	2005
	Real GDP (percent change)												
Fiji	2.6	5.1	2.5	4.7	-2.3	1.2	9.2	-2.8	2.7	4.3	3.0	4.1	2.1
Kiribati	1.5	8.4	5.2	3.8	1.9	12.6	9.5	1.6	1.9	-4.2	2.2	-1.4	0.3
Marshall Islands	2.5	3.9	3.8	-13.9	-11.5	-1.8	0.6	0.9	5.5	4.0	1.8	0.4	3.5
Micronesia	6.7	2.0	1.6	-5.1	-6.1	-0.7	-3.1	9.1	—	1.7	4.2	-3.5	1.3
Palau	-9.1	2.6	10.0	10.5	4.3	2.2	-3.4	0.3	1.3	-3.5	-1.3	4.9	5.5
Papua New Guinea	18.2	5.9	-3.3	7.7	-3.9	-3.8	7.6	-1.2	-0.1	-0.2	2.9	2.9	3.0
Samoa	5.3	6.4	6.6	7.3	0.8	1.1	2.1	6.1	7.1	4.4	1.8	3.5	4.0
Solomon Islands	4.0	9.2	8.2	1.6	-1.4	1.8	-0.5	-14.3	-9.0	-2.4	5.6	5.5	4.4
Tonga	3.7	4.3	4.6	0.3	-3.0	3.6	2.3	5.6	1.8	2.1	2.9	1.5	2.5
Vanuatu	4.5	1.3	7.4	2.5	8.6	4.3	-3.2	2.7	-2.7	-4.6	2.4	4.0	3.0
	Consumer prices (percent change)												
Fiji	5.2	0.6	2.2	4.9	3.4	5.9	2.0	1.1	4.3	0.8	4.2	2.8	3.7
Kiribati (end of period)	6.1	4.0	4.1	-1.5	2.2	4.7	0.4	1.0	7.3	1.1	1.6	-0.6	0.5
Marshall Islands	7.6	4.9	6.8	10.5	5.8	2.9	1.9	0.9	1.8	-0.4	-0.9	2.0	3.5
Micronesia	3.0	2.6	2.8	2.8	2.7	1.6	1.9	2.0	1.3	-0.1	-0.2	2.0	3.5
Palau	3.0	2.6	2.8	2.9	2.3	1.6	2.2	3.0	0.8	-1.2	-0.6	5.8	2.7
Papua New Guinea	5.0	2.9	17.3	11.6	3.9	13.6	14.9	15.6	9.3	11.8	14.7	2.1	2.8
Samoa (end of period)	1.7	12.1	-2.9	5.4	6.9	4.1	-0.6	2.7	1.1	9.8	1.6	17.2	-2.9
Solomon Islands	9.2	13.1	9.8	11.8	8.0	12.3	8.0	6.9	7.6	9.4	10.1	6.9	6.6
Tonga	1.8	3.9	-0.5	2.7	2.0	3.0	3.9	5.3	6.9	10.4	11.1	11.8	9.9
Vanuatu	3.6	2.3	2.2	0.9	2.8	3.3	2.2	2.5	3.7	2.0	3.0	1.4	1.0
	Central government balances (in percent of GDP)[2]												
Fiji	-4.7	-2.6	-1.7	-2.8	-4.0	-4.0	-1.2	-3.2	-6.5	-7.0	-6.0	-3.3	-3.8
Kiribati	0.4	-1.5	-10.2	-35.9	6.4	18.7	-5.8	-2.0	-17.0	-0.6	-31.9	-42.8	-22.6
Marshall Islands	...	...	-21.3	18.5	9.1	15.5	10.6	9.2	8.2	-4.0	11.0	-0.4	-2.1
Micronesia	-4.6	-0.3	-1.5	0.2	0.4	-7.1	-8.2	-6.7	-8.9	6.8	7.9	-4.8	-3.2
Palau	-0.3	-0.5	105.4	-10.3	-16.8	-0.1	-18.0	-15.6	-20.3	-28.3	-2.4	-6.9	-3.9
Papua New Guinea	-6.0	0.1	-1.3	-3.4	-3.6	-0.4	-4.5	-1.3	-3.9	-5.3	-1.6	1.1	1.9
Samoa	-12.8	-7.8	-2.9	0.9	1.0	2.0	0.3	-0.7	-2.3	-2.1	-0.6	-0.9	-0.6

Table 1.1 *(continued)*

	1993	1994	1995	1996	1997	1998	1999	2000	2001	2002	2003	2004	2005
Solomon Islands	...	...	-4.8	-3.9	-4.3	1.0	-3.3	-7.8	-12.7	-11.0	-1.9	8.3	-0.5
Tonga	...	...	-3.6	0.9	-4.8	-2.3	-0.2	-0.3	-1.5	-1.5	-3.1	1.3	0.1
Vanuatu	-3.8	-1.6	-2.8	-1.9	-0.5	-6.7	-0.6	-7.0	-3.7	-4.1	-1.7	0.9	1.0
Central government revenue and grants (in percent of GDP)[2]													
Fiji	24.5	24.9	24.4	23.9	24.6	24.5	25.1	24.2	22.1	24.6	25.1	25.8	25.8
Kiribati	99.1	90.8	93.6	75.7	125.6	135.5	105.8	98.9	118.4	138.7	139.2	106.2	123.2
Marshall Islands	...	...	73.9	80.5	74.6	74.7	67.6	75.2	70.1	64.2	65.0	56.2	58.1
Micronesia	82.5	81.5	81.9	80.2	70.9	76.6	76.6	68.5	64.2	71.8	71.8	53.7	51.0
Palau	63.7	60.8	178.8	59.4	49.6	59.1	41.8	52.6	43.1	42.4	54.0	54.3	53.6
Papua New Guinea	27.4	27.6	28.1	28.4	31.6	29.2	28.8	31.2	29.7	27.8	28.2	31.1	28.1
Samoa	44.4	42.2	47.6	46.8	39.5	36.1	40.0	34.4	31.9	33.8	32.8	32.5	40.0
Solomon Islands	...	...	35.6	34.7	28.9	29.0	27.0	22.1	23.5	18.8	37.6	48.9	48.5
Tonga	...	...	43.8	31.7	31.5	28.4	24.6	26.4	27.5	29.9	27.3	27.5	26.0
Vanuatu	23.1	24.9	27.8	24.8	23.1	21.8	25.8	22.1	20.9	21.0	20.1	21.9	22.2
Central government expenditure and net lending (in percent of GDP)[2]													
Fiji	29.2	27.5	26.1	26.7	28.6	28.5	26.3	27.4	28.6	31.6	31.1	29.1	29.6
Kiribati	98.8	92.3	103.8	111.7	119.2	116.7	111.6	100.9	135.4	139.3	171.0	149.0	145.8
Marshall Islands	...	...	95.2	62.0	65.5	59.2	57.1	66.0	61.9	68.2	54.0	56.6	60.2
Micronesia	87.0	81.8	83.3	80.0	70.5	83.8	84.8	75.2	73.1	65.0	63.8	58.6	54.2
Palau	60.1	61.7	70.7	72.1	68.8	55.9	63.0	72.8	64.6	66.3	62.6	61.7	54.2
Papua New Guinea	36.3	30.6	27.7	26.7	32.2	30.9	33.4	32.3	33.2	31.8	29.4	29.6	26.2
Samoa	57.1	50.0	52.5	45.9	38.3	34.1	39.6	35.1	34.3	35.9	33.4	33.4	40.6
Solomon Islands	...	...	40.4	38.6	33.2	28.0	30.3	29.9	36.2	29.8	39.5	40.6	49.0
Tonga	...	...	47.4	30.7	36.3	30.7	24.8	26.8	29.0	31.3	30.4	26.2	25.8
Vanuatu	26.8	26.5	30.6	26.7	23.7	28.4	26.4	29.0	24.6	25.0	21.8	21.0	21.2

Current account balance (in percent of GDP)

Fiji	-1.0	-1.1	0.6	2.3	1.8	1.5	-7.1	-7.4	-3.5	-1.7	-2.0	-5.0	-4.5
Kiribati	12.5	3.5	3.1	-12.1	-22.0	35.2	12.4	13.1	2.0	-1.8	-19.3	-16.3	-9.4
Marshall Islands	9.4	3.3	-21.6	-8.3	-0.7	3.3	-7.9	4.7	8.8	8.6	16.3	4.4	0.5
Micronesia	-1.9	0.2	11.3	8.2	-10.5	-3.5	2.4	0.3	-5.4	7.3	0.9	-10.6	-12.1
Palau	11.2	10.7	74.4	8.6	12.4	20.6	-54.5	-30.6	-9.4	-11.0	9.6	12.6	15.1
Papua New Guinea	12.6	11.1	19.2	5.5	-5.4	0.6	2.8	8.7	6.5	-1.0	4.4	2.1	4.0
Samoa	-19.4	1.9	4.8	5.0	-3.6	9.5	2.0	1.0	0.1	-0.6	2.9	4.4	2.2
Solomon Islands	-2.6	0.4	7.1	6.9	-5.6	-1.6	3.1	-10.6	-12.8	-7.2	1.3	12.5	-10.8
Tonga	3.0	-11.2	-11.0	-5.9	-0.9	-10.5	-0.6	-5.9	-9.2	4.9	-3.0	4.0	-2.2
Vanuatu	-1.1	-3.1	-2.0	-2.1	-0.8	2.7	-5.2	2.0	2.0	-9.0	-10.2	-9.5	-7.1

Gross reserves (in months of imports)

Fiji	3.3	2.9	3.7	4.0	3.8	4.8	4.2	4.6	4.3	3.5	3.1	3.3	3.5
Papua New Guinea	1.6	0.9	3.1	5.4	3.3	2.0	2.1	3.2	5.7	4.5	5.6	5.8	5.1
Samoa	4.5	5.4	4.6	5.4	5.9	5.4	6.3	4.5	3.6	4.2	3.4	3.5	3.9
Solomon Islands	1.1	0.8	0.8	1.6	1.9	3.6	4.6	3.1	2.8	2.1	3.6	5.7	4.7
Tonga	6.4	4.3	3.1	3.4	3.7	1.7	3.7	2.4	1.8	2.8	2.0	4.8	4.0
Vanuatu	...	...	...	3.9	3.6	3.3	3.5	3.1	5.2	4.3	4.3	4.8	4.9

External debt (in percent of GDP)

Fiji	17.8	15.5	13.5	12.1	11.5	13.6	14.0	14.7	13.6	13.7	12.2	10.9	11.1
Kiribati	19.5	20.8	18.3	18.0	18.0	15.3	15.5	16.3	20.0	16.4	16.0	17.5	19.0
Marshall Islands	155.1	170.9	144.5	134.9	135.7	130.2	101.8	93.3	77.0	70.6	71.2	76.4	70.6
Micronesia	71.8	63.8	56.5	50.3	50.0	47.8	42.8	30.7	26.3	25.6	25.2	25.8	24.8
Palau	...	...	16.8	11.9	8.1	4.7	1.2	17.2	16.2	16.6	15.9	14.0	13.2
Papua New Guinea	27.2	26.4	33.0	27.0	26.6	35.6	42.0	42.8	48.7	51.5	43.8	34.3	27.7
Samoa	89.7	93.3	89.9	78.0	65.6	62.6	66.1	63.0	61.4	62.0	59.6	51.5	48.1
Solomon Islands	32.6	30.1	28.9	29.0	30.0	37.7	39.3	42.0	49.0	67.0	70.6	62.0	61.4
Tonga	35.9	34.0	38.8	35.2	41.2	34.5	39.1	39.0	40.4	46.3	43.9	40.9	35.6
Vanuatu	21.6	21.7	21.2	18.9	17.3	20.8	22.2	28.2	29.7	28.2	26.1	24.6	23.4

Table 1.1 *(concluded)*

	1993	1994	1995	1996	1997	1998	1999	2000	2001	2002	2003	2004	2005
					Exchange rates (national currency per US$, period average)[3]								
Fiji (F$)	1.54	1.46	1.41	1.40	1.44	1.99	1.97	2.12	2.28	2.18	1.89	1.73	1.68
Kiribati ($A)	1.47	1.37	1.35	1.28	1.34	1.59	1.55	1.72	1.93	1.84	1.53	1.36	1.30
Marshall Islands (US$)	1.00	1.00	1.00	1.00	1.00	1.00	1.00	1.00	1.00	1.00	1.00	1.00	1.00
Micronesia (US$)	1.00	1.00	1.00	1.00	1.00	1.00	1.00	1.00	1.00	1.00	1.00	1.00	1.00
Palau (US$)	1.00	1.00	1.00	1.00	1.00	1.00	1.00	1.00	1.00	1.00	1.00	1.00	1.00
Papua New Guinea (K)	0.98	1.01	1.28	1.32	1.44	2.06	2.54	2.76	3.37	3.88	3.54	3.22	3.10
Samoa (SAT)	2.57	2.53	2.47	2.46	2.56	2.77	3.02	3.11	3.44	3.47	3.19	2.86	2.70
Solomon Islands (SI$)	3.19	3.29	3.41	3.57	4.75	4.82	4.84	5.10	5.56	7.46	7.49	7.51	7.52
Tonga (T$)	1.37	1.37	1.28	1.26	1.23	1.35	1.58	1.64	1.97	2.18	2.19	2.04	1.94
Vanuatu (VT)	121.58	116.41	112.11	111.72	115.87	127.52	129.08	137.64	145.31	139.10	122.20	111.90	109.05

Sources: National authorities; IMF, International Financial Statistics; and IMF staff estimates and projections.

[1]Marshall Islands, Federated States of Micronesia, and Palau—fiscal year ending September 30; Samoa and Tonga—fiscal year ending June 30; fiscal year data are shown in the ending calendar year.

[2]Micronesia: consolidated government. Palau: balance figures do not include errors and omissions.

[3]Figures in 2005 are as of end-October.

all countries must make a much greater commitment to accelerate structural reforms in order to improve public sector efficiency, create private sector employment opportunities, and alleviate poverty. Samoa is the most advanced in the reform process, which has been under way there for the past decade, and the benefits are now increasingly evident in higher investment, including foreign direct investment. Fiji is also attracting considerable foreign investment in the tourism sector. However, in most other parts of the region, there has been minimal interest in investment from abroad because of highly cumbersome and restrictive administrative regulations.

The regional approach of the Pacific Plan is appropriate for assisting the Pacific island countries in overcoming many of these challenges, because these countries continue to share many economic characteristics. They are all small in terms of GDP and population (see Table 1.2). They have narrow productive sectors based on primary commodities, with little diversification into manufacturing. Fiscal pressures limit the effectiveness of monetary policy. They have few export products, high import penetration shares, and are vulnerable to terms of trade fluctuations. They are also subject to frequent natural disasters, especially typhoons. Most of the countries have now prepared their own medium-term development strategies, which incorporate measures to promote fiscal consolidation and lower public debt burdens, to introduce more modern monetary policy frameworks, to ensure sound financial systems, and to create more favorable business climates. However, there is an urgent need to incorporate into these national plans more specific and integrated policy advice, including to ensure their consistency with medium-term fiscal strategies. The regional approach can help some of these countries overcome any lack of technical skills and institutional capacity to formulate and implement appropriate economic and financial policies.

The remaining chapters in this book examine in more detail some of the regional and country-specific challenges to achieving faster and sustainable economic growth. The book comprises two parts. Part I covers a number of pressing regional issues. Chapter 2 reviews the past dominance of the public sector in the countries of the region and the revenue and public expenditure management reforms that will be required to address the resultant fiscal pressures. Chapter 3 assesses the limited role of the private sector in the region and outlines a number of measures to reduce impediments to developing modern market economies and thereby achieving faster rates of growth. As noted, Chapter 4 examines the Pacific Plan, particularly the initiatives to promote growth, sustainable development, good governance, and security, as well as the mechanisms for monitoring

Table 1.2. Pacific Island Countries: Basic Economic and Social Characteristics

	Population (Thousands)	Area (In thousands of square kilometers)	Year of Independence	Year of Fund Membership	Institutional Inheritance	Main Regional Link
Fiji	840	18.3	1970	1971	United Kingdom	Australia
Kiribati	90	0.7	1971	1986	United Kingdom	Australia
Marshall Islands	58	0.2	1986	1992	United States	United States
Micronesia	108	0.7	1986	1993	United States	United States
Palau	20	0.5	1994	1997	United States	United States
Papua New Guinea	5,600	461.7	1975	1975	Australia	Australia
Samoa	181	2.8	1962	1971	New Zealand	New Zealand
Solomon Islands	471	28.0	1978	1978	United Kingdom	Australia
Tonga	101	0.7	1970	1985	United Kingdom	New Zealand
Vanuatu	215	12.2	1980	1981	United Kingdom; France	Australia

	GDP (US$ millions)	GDP per Capita (US$)	IMF Quota (SDR millions)	Consultation Cycle (Months)	Main Current Receipts (Remittances from private sector)	Exchange Rate Regime
Fiji	2,624	2,195	70.3	24	Sugar textiles, tourism	Basket peg
Kiribati	66	751	5.6	24	Fish licenses, seamen remittances	Australian dollar
Marshall Islands	144	2,559	3.5	24	Remittances from United States	U.S. dollar
Micronesia	239	2,211	5.1	24	Remittances from United States	U.S. dollar
Palau	134	6,482	3.1	24	Tourism	U.S. dollar
Papua New Guinea	4,000	714	131.6	12	Oil, copper, gold, coffee, cocoa	Float
Samoa	316	1,672	11.6	24	Remittances from New Zealand	Basket peg
Solomon Islands	258	550	10.4	12	Timber, palm oil, fish	Basket peg
Tonga	165	1,629	6.9	12	Remittances from New Zealand	Basket peg
Vanuatu	317	1,493	17.0	24	Tourism	Basket peg

	Aid per Capita (U.S. dollars)	Life Expectancy (Years)	Infant Mortality (Per 1,000 live births)	Population Growth (Percent per annum)	Health Spending (Percent of GDP)	Education Spending (Percent of GDP)
Fiji	61	70	16	0.9	4.2	5.6
Kiribati	191	63	49	2.1	8.0	4.9
Marshall Islands	991	65	53	3.5	10.6	16.4
Micronesia	923	69	19	0.6	6.5	7.0
Palau	1,295	70	23	0.7	9.1	11.0
Papua New Guinea	40	57	69	2.1	4.3	2.3
Samoa	186	70	19	0.8	6.2	4.8
Solomon Islands	132	70	19	2.6	4.8	3.5
Tonga	270	71	15	0.4	6.9	5.0
Vanuatu	154	69	31	2.0	3.8	11.0

Sources: World Bank, 2005 World Development Indicators; United Nations Development Programme; and World Health Organization.

and evaluating implementation of the Plan. Chapter 5 outlines the economic issues related to migration and remittances from migrant workers, which in some countries represent a stable source of foreign exchange and play an important role in reducing the economic vulnerability of individuals. Chapter 6 compares the Pacific island economies with those of the developing island countries in the Eastern Caribbean Currency Union (ECCU), drawing lessons from the more successful development policies and experiences of the latter. Chapter 7 examines possible alternatives for exchange rate arrangements in the Pacific island countries, taking into account that their small size and open economies leave them vulnerable to external shocks. Chapters 8–17, which comprise Part II of the book, examine the specific economic and policy challenges facing the 10 IMF member countries in the region.

2

Public Sector Activities

CHRISTOPHER BROWNE AND EDIMON GINTING

Large and pervasive public sectors characterize the Pacific island countries. Despite the fact that low levels of private sector activity limit the domestic tax bases, budgetary receipts in relation to GDP are substantial compared to other countries with similar levels of income per capita. For several countries this reflects nontax revenues, especially from fishing fees, but for most countries, this reflects the very high levels of external grants that are typically channeled through the public sector. Current expenditure is also large in relation to GDP, reflecting primarily high wage and salary bills, as well as financial support for public enterprises. Public investment is sizable, although it is almost entirely financed with external concessional assistance. Governance is an important issue throughout the region, especially in ensuring expenditure control.

Most countries in the region inherited a conservative approach to budgetary management upon independence in the 1970s and 1980s. For several years thereafter, fiscal policy aimed to achieve approximate budgetary balance over the medium term, in recognition that a more expansionary policy stance could contribute to balance of payments pressures. The avoidance of fiscal deficits depended crucially on maintaining the buoyancy of receipts and tight control over expenditures, although some countries experienced difficulties in restraining spending.

From the mid-1990s, more widespread fiscal pressures emerged, and most of the Pacific island countries recorded budget deficits. Marshall Islands and Micronesia found it difficult to adjust fully to step-downs in the level of Compact funding from the United States, and had only limited success in reducing their public sector wage bills.[1] In Papua New Guinea, political uncertainties contributed during several periods to the lack of fiscal discipline. In Solomon Islands, substantial payments were made to militants through the budget during and after the period of civil conflict that broke out in mid-1999. Fiji sharply increased overall spending, with a view to promoting economic recovery following a military coup in 2000. Kiribati greatly expanded spending from about 2003, drawing heavily on its external reserve assets. The only important exception was Samoa, which has pursued a comprehensive economic reform program consistently since 1994.

This chapter focuses on the main fiscal policy challenges facing the Pacific islands that must be addressed to secure fiscal consolidation and satisfactory debt management. Specific actions to strengthen revenues and improve expenditure management should include: simplifying tariff regimes, including by reducing the level and number of rates; introducing a final withholding tax on wages and salaries; introducing a presumptive tax, based on turnover, for hard-to-tax small businesses or self-employed taxpayers; reducing the number of exemptions, particularly for the corporate income tax; eliminating tax holidays; instituting better debt management and general enforcement procedures; allocating adequate budget resources to tax operations; controlling public expenditure; redirecting spending toward health, education, and infrastructure; and implementing public expenditure management reform.

Fiscal Policy

The overriding objective of fiscal strategy is to promote economic growth while ensuring macroeconomic stability and careful debt management. This requires action in four key areas. The first is to enhance the efficiency of the tax system by improving administration, broadening the tax base, and reducing tax incentives. The second is to institute measures to limit the spillover to the fiscal accounts of highly variable nontax receipts, including longer-term agreements for fishing licenses. The third is to redirect spending from public sector wages and salaries to education,

---

[1]Both countries have been closely affiliated with the United States under the Compact of Free Association. Compact I, covering 1987–2001, provided grants to Micronesia that comprised about half of total GDP and to Marshall Islands at a similarly high level. Compact II, covering 2004–23, entails lower U.S. assistance.

health, and infrastructure. The fourth is to improve budget-monitoring techniques to closely track all types of spending. For all Pacific island countries, another important area is to ensure the effective use of donor funding: over the medium term, external concessionary support may trend downward, at least from some key donors, and all efforts should be made to demonstrate to donors that aid funds are being used effectively and should be continued to the greatest extent possible.

Although many of the Pacific island countries continue to face difficulties with achieving fiscal consolidation, there were dramatic improvements in the budgetary situations of Papua New Guinea and Solomon Islands in recent years. Papua New Guinea reduced its deficit from nearly 6 percent of GDP in 2002 to 1 percent in 2004, as a result of decisively tighter control of expenditures, as well as a boost to mineral tax revenue from strong commodity export prices. The overall budgetary balance in Solomon Islands moved from a deficit of 10 percent of GDP in 2002 to an estimated surplus of 10 percent in 2004, following increased grants from Australia and other donors after the restoration of law and order in mid-2003 and a marked improvement in budgeting discipline. However, external support is expected to run down in due course and, without firm adjustment policies, renewed fiscal pressures could emerge in these countries.

The size of the public sectors in the Pacific island countries will probably diminish only gradually relative to GDP in the coming years, notwithstanding efforts to strengthen private sector activity, because deep-seated structural impediments will prevent any rapid transformation of these economies. In such circumstances, prudent debt management policy is a vital element of fiscal strategy, and debt sustainability should be among the countries' medium-term objectives. Indebted countries such as Marshall Islands, Papua New Guinea, and Solomon Islands should steadily lower their domestic and external debt, as envisioned by the authorities, and should steadfastly avoid external commercial borrowing to finance the budget.

Several countries in the region have trust funds. Kiribati's approach is to limit drawdowns from the Revenue Equalization Reserve Fund in order to keep per capita assets constant, which is appropriate given that donor funds are generally available to finance worthwhile investment projects. Marshall Islands and Micronesia will need to steadily build up their Compact Trust Funds through budgetary surpluses to comply with Compact II, which envisions the end of U.S. grant assistance after 2023. It is crucial that they initiate the required fiscal adjustments without delay in order to meet these goals.

Table 2.1. Selected Pacific Island Countries: Structure of Tax Revenue in FY2002

(In percent of GDP)

	Fiji	Kiribati	Marshall Islands	Micronesia	Palau	Papua New Guinea	Samoa	Solomon Islands	Tonga	Vanuatu
Income	6.8	8.1	9.2	3.6	4.8	13.6	4.5	5.3	4.9	0.0
Goods and services	8.8	0.0	3.3	5.1	8.8	5.2	12.4	6.6	3.1	10.3
International trade	4.5	17.2	5.7	3.2	4.5	2.8	3.9	7.7	15.2	6.8
Other tax	0.1	0.1	1.0	0.4	0.0	0.0	0.5	0.0	0.1	0.0
Total tax revenue	20.2	25.5	19.2	12.3	18.1	21.6	21.2	19.9	23.3	17.2

Sources: National authorities and IMF staff estimates.

Revenue Issues

The countries in the region need to strengthen their revenue efforts to face several critical realities. First, many countries have been heavily dependent on external grants, which are projected to gradually decline relative to GDP. Second, they face declining receipts from natural resources, particularly from fishing license fees, which have constituted a large but inconsistent source of government receipts in Kiribati, Marshall Islands, Micronesia, Palau, Samoa, and Tonga. These countries should seek to secure longer-term contracts and to obtain a greater share of royalties from foreign fishing fleets. In Papua New Guinea, revenue from the mineral and petroleum sectors is expected to decline in coming years, even if world prices remain high, as a result of tax concessions and resource depletion. Finally, tariffs and other trade taxes remain an important revenue source, particularly for Kiribati, Solomon Islands, and Tonga (Table 2.1). However, the commitment to trade liberalization in the Plan and the reductions in tariffs to take place under the Pacific Island Countries Trade Agreement (PICTA) and the Pacific Agreement on Closer Economic Relations (PACER) both have the potential to steadily erode such revenues.

Faced with these prospects, there is a need to accelerate efforts to efficiently mobilize revenue. First, a number of countries in the region rely on relatively complex tax systems, and priority should be given to reforms that make the tax system simpler, especially in income tax arrangements. Second, the countries in the region need to improve tax administration to enhance compliance and collection across the board. Such efforts might include greater use of self-assessment procedures for income taxes, development of comprehensive audit programs, assignment of a single taxpayer identification number, development of modern computer systems to stream-line operations, and perhaps establishment of large taxpayer offices. Third, the tax base should be expanded in numerous countries in the region by reducing exemptions that are overly generous, especially for industrial park developments and foreign investment, which can be a source of corruption as they are generally nontransparent (Box 2.1). Only after these three tasks are completed should new tax opportunities be considered.

About half the countries of the region now have a value-added tax (VAT) or a consumption tax. During the 1990s, Fiji, Papua New Guinea, Samoa, and Vanuatu successfully implemented a VAT, with basic rates in the range of 10–12.5 percent, which helped compensate for the revenue lost through steady tariff reductions. Tonga introduced a consumption tax (similar to a VAT) in 2005. In general, the VAT has been reasonably administered in the region. However, administration could be improved by faster processing of rebates, improved compliance at ports (where most revenue is collected), and upgraded capacity for conducting audits. There may also be problems in some countries where the threshold is set too low so that businesses that do not keep detailed books of account are forced to pay the tax despite their inability to properly calculate their liabilities; a presumptive tax for them might be preferable.

Improvements in customs administration are needed to facilitate both trade and more efficient collection of customs revenues. Over the longer term, elimination of customs duties under the regional trade agreements (PACER and PICTA) and the increasing importance of a VAT or con-sumption tax will require improved procedures for collecting taxes on imports. Some of the larger economies, including Fiji, Papua New Guinea, and Samoa, have had automated customs systems in place for several years. Modernized procedures based on such automated systems have been newly implemented in Micronesia, are being implemented in Palau, and are planned for a number of the smaller countries in the region. Regional initiatives to this end should be supported, including through the Pacific Financial Technical Assistance Centre, the Pacific Forum, donors, and perhaps the Oceanic Custom Organization.

Expenditure Rationalization and Management Reforms

Public expenditure is quite high in the Pacific island countries, espe-cially in Kiribati, Marshall Islands, Micronesia, and Palau. Because of the difficulties associated with increasing revenues and the expected decline in donor assistance, expenditures will likely take the brunt of fiscal adjust-

Box 2.1. Tax Incentive Issues in Selected Pacific Island Countries

The principal policy and administrative weakness of the current tax systems lies in the proliferation of exemptions—both statutory and discretionary—which undermine integrity and revenue-raising potential. One of the most harmful features is the prevalence of income tax holidays that are of questionable value in promoting investment.

- Fiji: Incentives include investment allowances on capital expenditure in the agricultural, information technology, and hotel sectors; accelerated depreciation on buildings used for agricultural, commercial, and industrial purposes; tax holidays of 10–20 years for qualifying investments in the hotel sector; a deduction of one-and-a-half times the wages paid to qualifying employees; exemptions of export income at decreasing proportions until 2009; and a duty-suspension scheme for both duties and the VAT to exporters who import inputs to be used in production of exports.
- Kiribati: At least 20 percent of imports (by value) is exempted. Most forgone customs duties come from the government (60 percent), aid projects (18 percent), and diplomatic missions (10 percent).
- Papua New Guinea: Tax incentives operate at three levels. First, incentives are granted to a number of large companies in several sectors (mainly mining and oil). Second, incentives are granted to specific companies in targeted sectors, such as export-oriented activities and agriculture. Third, there are immediate deductions for some other private sector activities, including deduction of 20 percent of the cost of investment, free depreciation for manufacturers who install industrial plants, 100 percent exemption from income tax of net income attributable to export sales, and full deduction of certain investment expenditures for primary producers.
- Solomon Islands: Incentive packages may be granted, including a 3- to 6-year tax holiday for manufacturing and export-oriented manufactures; a 5- to 10-year tax holiday for investment for approved overseas promotions fostering tourism; concessions for export businesses involved in agricultural produce, manufactured or processed goods, or fresh seafood; and additional incentives for capital expenditures on new or expanded factory space.
- Tonga: There are many exemptions for government, quasi-governmental bodies, and the private sector under the Development Incentives Act. About 30 percent of the value of government imports and 37 percent of quasi-governmental imports were exempted.
- Vanuatu: Discretionary tax exemptions are granted to selected industries, with the director of customs holding final decision-making power to grant exemptions. Goods eligible for possible exemption include imports for manufacture, agriculture, horticulture, forestry, inter-island shipping, tourism development projects, mineral exploration and extraction, fisheries, and other development projects.

ment. Strong action is needed to improve the quality of expenditure throughout the region, in order to contain fiscal pressures, increase fiscal flexibility, and promote higher growth. Governments must implement over the medium term reforms to improve the productivity of public spending, promote governance and transparency, reduce subsidies, avoid crowding out the private sector, and strengthen expenditure controls. The optimal composition of government expenditure will differ in each country, depending on the structure of the economy, the requisite service delivery, and the relative costs of inputs.

Public Sector Wages and Salaries

In most countries of the region, public expenditure is dominated by current spending, a large proportion of which goes to public service wages. Although no dramatic, sudden changes are expected in the size of the public sector in these countries, maintenance of the status quo will not contribute to faster sustainable growth. There are obvious political sensitivities in downsizing the public sector, especially in light of the limited private sector employment opportunities, but it is important that incremental progress is made in this area.

A number of countries have promoted efforts over the past decade to reduce their civil service wage bills. This issue is especially important for Marshall Islands, Micronesia, and Palau, where the government wage bill is 20–25 percent of GDP, although the wage and salary bills are also high in other countries, at about 10–12 percent of GDP. Marshall Islands implemented a Public Sector Reform Program in 1996, following the step-down in Compact funding, which focused on reducing the public payroll, but these steps were subsequently reversed by an increase in wage rates. Micronesia cut the public wage bill in the context of a similar program during 1996–99, but these changes were also partly reversed. Papua New Guinea has made some progress in improving payroll administration, identifying ghost workers, and eliminating overpayment of allowances, and the government has announced a strategic plan for public sector reform, focused on downsizing the public sector by 10 percent by 2007. It is also committed to implement the recommendations contained in the World Bank–led Public Expenditure Review and Rationalization report, but much remains to be done. Solomon Islands is now restructuring the public sector with the help of external advisors.

Health, Education, and Infrastructure

Successful efforts to reduce less productive expenditure, including the wage bill, could enhance the scope for redirecting spending toward health, education, and infrastructure without undermining fiscal consolidation. This is important to promote longer-term sustainable growth, raise the skills of the workforce, and encourage private sector activities. While social indicators, such as life expectancy, literacy, and infant mortality, have improved in recent years in the region, overall standards remain disappointing, especially given the substantial aid programs directed to these matters.

Public Expenditure Management Reforms

Effective expenditure adjustments need to be supported by institutional reforms to improve the quality of public expenditure throughout the region. Closer links are required between the annual budgeting exercise and medium-term development strategies. At present, forward estimates of expenditure, when undertaken, tend to be unrealistic, especially the (under)estimates of operating and maintenance costs for capital projects. Budget formulation tends to be incremental and expansionary, whereas lasting expenditure reduction must be driven by a comprehensive review rather than piecemeal cuts.

There is a strong need to improve expenditure control and accountability mechanisms. Capacity building is essential to establish and manage appropriate internal control systems. Internal audits should be strengthened, and greater attention should be given to better and more timely reporting. Where appropriate, emphasis should be given to eliminating existing arrears and avoiding new arrears.

Samoa has made progress over the past decade a part of its comprehensive structural reform process, and this has enhanced both its recent growth rate and its prospects for achieving sustainable high growth over the medium term. Government current spending was reduced sharply and has remained low by regional standards, and sustained reforms were implemented in government financial management. Output budgeting was applied to all departments, and the government budget now provides detail on performance in order to assess the accountability and efficiency of government spending.

A number of other Pacific island countries have recently launched public financial management reform. However, implementation progress has been limited due to weak domestic capacities and governance issues. Fiji has renewed its commitment to financial management reform, in view of the escalating budget deficits since the 2000 coup and the difficult structural issues that need to be addressed in the textile and sugar industries. Papua New Guinea is strengthening its expenditure control systems to implement best international practice standards.

Public Enterprises

In most countries of the region, the government is closely involved in commercial activities. Public enterprises operate in areas that in most countries are left to the private sector, such as wholesale and retail trade, hotels, agriculture, fisheries, shipping, and airlines. The financial condition of most state-owned enterprises remains weak, and public enterprises have added to budgetary pressures. High wage costs, overstaffing, and management problems in the state-owned enterprises have been common. For public utilities, problems have often arisen from insufficiently flexible utility pricing policies.

Efforts to limit budgetary subsidy contributions to public enterprises are crucial. Privatization should be pursued, where feasible, but there may be limited interest among investors in loss-making enterprises, especially in the smaller Pacific island countries. To support efforts to reduce the size of the public sector, governments should avoid new spending initiatives for public enterprises, especially in industrial and commercial areas, and should leave such investment to the private sector whenever possible. For example, the joint airline arrangements with foreign carriers now in place for Samoa, Tonga, and Vanuatu should help limit budgetary costs.

Conclusions

The Pacific island countries must strengthen revenues and improve expenditure management in order to ensure fiscal consolidation and satisfactory debt management. As discussed in this chapter, these efforts should include simplifying tariff regimes; improving the efficiency of tax systems; allocating adequate budget resources to tax operations; instituting better debt management; controlling public expenditure; redirecting spending toward health, education, and infrastructure; and implementing public expenditure management reform.

3

Private Sector Development

CHRISTOPHER BROWNE AND JONG KYU LEE

Private sector activity in the Pacific island countries is a small share of GDP and has increased only modestly in recent years. The private sector faces many impediments, including the small size and remoteness of these economies, crowding out of the private sector by the public sector, distortions in resource allocation, political instability, governance problems, and a lack of the institutions needed to facilitate growth of a modern market economy. This chapter outlines the main problems that need to be addressed to reduce impediments to achieve a faster rate of growth in the region and identifies possible ways to move ahead.

The Role of the Private Sector

Most countries in the region are dependent on the primary and tertiary sectors of the economy as the main sources of output. The shares of mining and manufacturing in GDP are generally under 10 percent, except in Fiji (which has a garment industry), Papua New Guinea (mining sector), and Samoa (auto parts). The services sector (including the large government sector) contributes 40–85 percent of GDP, while the agricultural sector provides 10–33 percent (higher in Solomon Islands) (Table 3.1). Since 1990, the share of the agricultural sector has decreased in most countries while that of the service sector has increased; the min-

Table 3.1. Sectoral Output in Selected Pacific Island Countries
(In percent of GDP)

	1990			2002[1]		
	Agriculture	Mining and manu-facturing	Services	Agriculture	Mining and manu-facturing	Services
Fiji	20.4	17.0	62.6	15.4	16.9	68.4
Kiribati	21.9	1.2	76.9	12.8	1.4	85.9
Marshall Islands	13.9	1.4	84.7	10.4	4.8	84.8
Papua New Guinea	28.9	23.7	47.4	33.1	26.7	39.5
Samoa	23.0	19.6	57.4	15.3	16.2	68.5
Solomon Islands	46.4	4.6	49.0	47.7	4.1	48.2
Tonga	34.7	6.4	58.8	30.2	5.7	64.1
Vanuatu	20.7	5.5	73.8	15.6	3.5	80.9

Source: Asian Development Bank.
[1]Earlier in some cases.

ing and manufacturing sectors have remained small, with only limited diversification.

Notwithstanding substantial external grant assistance, which typically amounts to 10–20 percent of GDP and is primarily used for development spending, overall investment ratios are relatively modest. In Fiji, Papua New Guinea, and Tonga, investment rates have declined over the past decade to about 20 percent of GDP, and to 15 percent of GDP in Vanuatu, compared with an average investment ratio of above 29 percent of GDP for all developing countries. Foreign direct investment is modest, with its ratio to GDP below 10 percent for all countries.

Credit to the private sector is also modest and has been stable or decreasing in recent years. The ratio of credit to the private sector to GDP in 2002 was 29 percent for Fiji, 12 percent for Papua New Guinea, 42 percent for Tonga, and 41 percent for Vanuatu. By way of comparison, the ratio was 61 percent in Mauritius and has increased in recent years. To a considerable extent, the low investment rates and credit share reflect the underdevelopment of the private sector.

As a consequence of this lack of production diversification, the Pacific island countries are very open economies. The share of imports in GDP reaches 80 percent in Kiribati, 65 percent in Tonga, and about 50 percent in Fiji and Marshall Islands. The lowest ratios are in Solomon Islands and Papua New Guinea, although even here the import ratios are about 30 percent of GDP. Export shares are particularly high in Fiji, Papua New Guinea, and Solomon Islands, but lower in the other countries. The resulting large trade deficits are normally covered by large worker remittances and official development flows.

Impediments to Private Sector Growth

The Natural Environment

The Pacific island countries are small in size, remote, and subject to frequent natural disasters, all of which lead to considerable volatility in economic activity. Except for Papua New Guinea, all of the countries have populations under 1 million, and several have populations of less than 100,000. The smallest IMF member is Palau, with a population of only about 19,000. These countries' size provides a natural limit to their range of business activity and the potential for economic growth by constraining domestic markets, economies of scale, and competition.

These countries' remoteness also limits the potential for trade and growth. They are located far from their major markets, namely Australia, New Zealand, and Asia. Given the small trade volumes, this distance causes unit transportation costs to be high, making it difficult to maintain regular shipments, which in turn leads to additional costs of inventory. Furthermore, most Pacific island countries are comprised of island groups dispersed over a wide area. Distances between islands make internal transportation services expensive and infrequent.

Land Issues and Property Rights

The lack of formal property rights, particularly for land, hampers business activities and economic development (Box 3.1). Extended family members normally co-own their properties and share the harvests. At the village level, members in a village share their production, which obscures property rights. Such communal ownership precludes the economic use of land, binding rural land to subsistence agriculture rather than commercial-type cultivation. Furthermore, it makes it difficult to sell land because all members of the extended family must agree to the sale. In addition, land cannot be used as collateral for loans, and disputes and conflict over land are common, which increases uncertainty for businesses.

Skilled Labor Constraints

The relatively large size of government in these countries reduces the availability of skilled labor for the private sector. In Marshall Islands and Micronesia, public sector wage rates are estimated to be double those in the private sector. Minimum wages are also high compared with other countries in Asia.

Box 3.1. Aspects of Traditional Land Tenure in the Pacific Region

Legal Aspects: Most land arrangements are influenced by custom, tenure, and laws. Almost all tenure was guided only by traditional customs and precedents until the last century. The establishment of central governments brought about the passage of laws to govern land use, and these now exist alongside customary rules, although the emphasis remains on communal ownership.

Acquisition of Land: Land rights are traditionally acquired at birth, rather than through the sale and acquisition of land, and this remains the most common pattern of access to land.

Ownership Rights to Land: Rights to land are multiple, conditional, and negotiable. No rights are absolute. Rights of males differ from (and are generally superior to) rights of females. Rights of older brothers and cousins of more senior lines are often superior to those of juniors. Resident right holders take precedence, other things being equal, over nonresidents. Labor strengthens land rights; for example, those who work the land enhance their claims over those of equal blood right who do not. Forceful personalities and persuasive arguments can tilt the balance, because multiple principles can be called upon in disputes and varying degrees of emphasis can be given to them to benefit one party or another.

Accessibility to Land: Every household needs access to several kinds of land for different purposes. Even though land plots are narrow slices, almost all the people in the community have rights to more than one slice because that facilitates exchange of use rights with others in a complex pattern of mutual obligation and reciprocity that broadens options and enhances social security.

Ownership of Land: No one person holds all rights to any plot of land. Individual rights are nested with those of extended families, lineages, clans, and tribes. Wives hold rights contingent on marriage. The land rights of an adoptee vary greatly, depending on the circumstances of the adoption and the relationship between the adopting parents and the adoptee. Refugees and

The lack of employment opportunities at home makes emigration common. About half the populations of Samoa and Tonga live overseas, especially in New Zealand. Many citizens of Marshall Islands, Micronesia, and Palau have taken advantage of their entitlement to live and work in the United States. Kiribati has a well-regarded merchant seaman training institute, which has enabled graduates to obtain long-term contracts with international shipping companies. Fiji suffered heavy permanent emigration of skilled workers of Indian descent following military coups in the 1980s and 1990s, especially to Australia and Canada. In addition, Fiji has others with special needs are often accommodated under negotiated arrangements, but the rights of refugees and adoptees are often vulnerable once the person who granted the rights dies.

Ruling over Land: Day-to-day decisions are based on broad customary principles modified by pragmatism, because different customs can be used to justify different actions. For example, seniority might in itself give priority over juniors, but persons with outstanding records of military or community service may rank higher. Because there is no writing or mapping, rights and boundaries rely on memory.

Transfer of Land Rights: Most land rights are transferred by inheritance from a parent or other close blood relative, but many factors come into play in the process. These include the needs of individuals, the harmony or conflict between potential heirs and heritors, the extent to which heirs have used the land, who provided for the elders in their declining years, and what payments were made at funerary feasts.

Registration of Land: Only a small portion of land has been registered. The fact of having been registered, however, does not mean that the registration is necessarily up to date. Registration and surveys are not necessarily linked. Furthermore, neither a registration nor a survey is useful unless the records are well protected and up to date. The fact that neither is done regularly has been a major problem in the region. In some instances, records have been destroyed through war. But the more common problems are ineffective administration, theft or forgery of records, and fire or hurricane damage. Loss or deterioration of records through mildew and storm damage, and deliberate falsifications are serious problems. In practice, many land records have not survived in a comprehensive and accurate form.

Source: Ron Crocombe, 1998, *Land Tenure in Pacific Developing Member Countries* (Manila: Asian Development Bank).

traditionally provided substantial numbers of military personnel for UN peacekeeping operations and is now providing contractors in the Middle East, including in Iraq.

One positive effect of emigration on the Pacific island countries is the inflow of remittances, which help to improve development prospects, maintain macroeconomic stability, mitigate the effects of external shocks, and reduce poverty. Remittances have increased human capital accumulation, through the financing of education and health care, increased investment in residential property, and the provision of funds to establish small businesses. Moreover, remittances have proved very resilient in the face of economic downturns in the region. Overall, however, emigration can create a vicious circle; when the best and most qualified workers leave, domestic business opportunities shrink further, which in turn encourages more skilled people to leave, and remittances may diminish the incentives to work for family members that remain.

State-Owned Enterprises

Most governments in the Pacific participate in commercial and industrial activities that in many other countries are carried out by the private sector. Throughout the region, electricity production and distribution, water and sewage services, telecommunication, ports, airlines and airports, and other types of infrastructure are operated by the government or by state-owned enterprises. In some countries, the government is also engaged in such conventional commercial activities as hotels and resorts, breweries, computer companies, and Internet services, among others. For instance, in Kiribati, the government engages in the manufacture of biscuits, the harvesting of seaweed, and in wholesale and retail trade; in Marshall Islands, the government owns the copra processing plant; and in Papua New Guinea, the government operates a motor vehicle insurance company. Several countries also have state-owned development banks, which generally make loans with less risk appraisal than commercial banks and which therefore have a large proportion of nonperforming loans.

The result of this extensive government involvement has been higher costs for private business due to large inefficiencies. For example, the absolute costs of electricity and telephone services are several times higher in the region than in Australia. Furthermore, the boards of directors of many private companies include members from the public sector or government, which does not necessarily help promote the best commercially oriented practices. Finally, preferential tax and customs treatment for public enterprises frequently creates unfair competition with the private sector.

The Regulatory Setting

Complicated rules and regulations govern business activities throughout the region, and many commercial and business laws are outdated or inappropriate. In Samoa, businesses operate on a law based on a New Zealand act from the 1960s, and in Papua New Guinea, the arbitration act dates from 1951. In addition, most laws were patterned after laws of countries with very different institutional frameworks.

The complexity of the laws (including rules and regulations) and a lack of clarity cause governance problems. A new business usually needs to obtain permits or licenses from several different government agencies. The laws are not adequately codified, which makes it difficult for businesses to know which laws and rules to follow, provides great scope for discretionary behavior by politicians and bureaucrats, and encourages corruption. There are no specialized commercial courts, and out-of-court arbitration and conciliation are rare, both of which increase the time and cost of resolving disputes. The inefficient legal framework can be a critical issue for foreign investors in particular.

Political Factors

Political instability in the region also hampers private business activity by creating an unsafe and insecure environment and by causing frequent or sudden changes in policy direction. In Fiji, there have been three military coups since the late 1980s, with trade sanctions by Australia and New Zealand and strengthened capital controls by the authorities in the wake of each coup, which has discouraged investment. In Papua New Guinea, no government has completed its five-year term since independence. In Solomon Islands, there was a period of ethnic conflict from mid-1999 through mid-2003. In the highland regions of Papua New Guinea, roadside bandits interrupt the marketing of agricultural crops such as coffee and cocoa, which has contributed to the collapse of large-scale farming. Political instability is attributable in part to social tensions and law-and-order problems that are accentuated by poor economic growth and the resulting lack of sufficient job opportunities.

Agenda for Private Sector Development

The Pacific island economies clearly face a number of geographical and environmental disadvantages and constraints. However, other countries that are small and isolated have nevertheless accomplished superior economic performance—for example, Mauritius. Further, despite limited land mass, the region has valuable natural resources, including fisheries and other marine resources, forests, arable land without noxious insects, and preserved areas suitable for ecotourism. To spur private sector growth and realize their economic potential, these countries must undertake comprehensive reforms, as outlined below.

Land Reform

Governments in the region need to examine the scope for land reform. In general, however, problems from the communal ownership of land can be overcome to some extent through changes to leasing contract arrangements, which at present are typically limited to 25 years. Where land reform is not feasible, governments might consider alternatives, such as provision of commercial space large enough for retail activities.

Public Sector Reforms

As discussed more fully in Chapter 2, the agenda for public sector reform should include measures to improve the competitive environment by eliminating preferential treatment of public enterprises. Wherever feasible, governments should withdraw from activities that can be undertaken more efficiently or effectively by the private sector and should focus on administering the regulatory system and managing supporting infrastructure. Steps to reduce corruption and improve governance within public enterprises are also vital to promote private sector activities. Reform of public enterprises in transportation should be given priority in order to minimize the distortions created by extensive government involvement in this sector, particularly since transportation costs are already high as a natural result of these countries' geographical isolation. Reducing the direct involvement of government in commercial aviation and shipping is important. However, the prospects for outright privatization of state enterprises may well be limited, especially in the smaller countries, because of the lack of investor interest.

Legal System Modernization

Efforts should be strengthened to modernize outdated legal systems, including updating commercially related laws and court procedures, creating individual property rights, and enabling the tradability of such rights. In addition, establishing one-step processes for gaining licenses and permits could reduce the high costs of doing business now associated with overly complex regulations, even though the best way to reduce these costs would be to reduce the overall number of regulations and requirements. To modernize laws, it would be desirable to consult with the private sector. Appropriate reforms in these directions could substantially reduce opportunities for bribery or corruption, which are harmful to private businesses.

Trade Liberalization

The Pacific island countries have recently concluded two agreements for trade liberalization. PACER, the Pacific Agreement on Closer Economic Relations, establishes guidelines for future development of trade relationships among them and provides the basis for closer economic cooperation with other countries, notably Australia and New Zealand. PICTA, the Pacific Island Countries Trade Agreement, contemplates the phaseout of most tariffs by 2009 for the larger islands and 2011 for the smaller islands. While the effects are expected to be modest and gradual, this liberalization process could also facilitate regional integration and private sector development.

4

The Pacific Plan for Strengthening Regional Cooperation and Integration

CHRISTOPHER BROWNE

Pacific Forum Economic Ministers called for a Pacific Plan for Strengthening Regional Cooperation and Integration at their April 2004 meeting in Auckland, New Zealand. They recognized that overcoming the serious challenges facing the region required sharing scarce resources and aligning policies to strengthen national capacities to support living standards. Following this agreement in principle, the concept was developed by the Pacific Islands Forum Secretariat (FORSEC) and discussed in detail with the island countries and major bilateral and multinational donors. The Plan was firmly supported by Australia and New Zealand. A comprehensive draft of the Plan for the upcoming 10-year period was approved by the Pacific Forum Economic Ministers at their June 2005 meeting in Tuvalu. A final version of the Plan was approved by the Pacific Islands Forum leaders at their October 2005 meeting in Papua New Guinea.[1]

The Plan identifies a strategic framework of regional policies to be achieved over various time horizons. Early practical issues are to be completed or initiated within three years, medium-term proposals within five years, and longer-term matters within 10 years. The proposed activities address, in an appropriate manner, the need to promote economic growth, sustainable development, good governance and security, private sector activities, public enterprise reforms, regional economic integration, and

---

[1]For further details on the history and details of the Pacific Plan, see www.pacificplan.org.

trade liberalization. The Plan also incorporates a wide range of highly ambitious regional initiatives to promote greater income equality, enhance gender and youth empowerment, and create regional bodies for air and sea transport rationalization, protection of intellectual property, auditing, ombudsmen, human rights, and peacekeeping. It will be difficult to make rapid progress in such areas.

Regionalism under the Plan does not imply any limitations on national sovereignty. It is not intended to replace any national programs, only to support and complement them. To facilitate successful implementation of the Plan, which in the first instance will be the responsibility of FORSEC, detailed implementation and monitoring and evaluation strategies have been developed for the first three years, with realistic objectives and outputs and clearly defined coordination responsibilities. There is to be sufficient flexibility to further the goal of regional integration. The main institutions to be involved in the day-to-day Plan implementation include national and regional economic planning and development departments, and treasury and finance officials from the island countries. Updated annual action plans will be prepared by the FORSEC for discussion at future Pacific Forum Economic Ministers' meetings.

The Plan underscores the commitment of the Pacific island countries to actively pursue measures to stimulate economic growth and poverty reduction. The Plan recognizes that overall economic performance in the region has deteriorated since independence two or three decades ago. It acknowledges that large public sectors, governance issues, corruption, and failure to promote the private sector have contributed to this outcome and that all these issues need to be addressed. With regard to the medium-term outlook, lifting the growth record requires the pursuit of broad economic reforms and continued bilateral and multilateral support. In this regard, the Plan provides a well-thought-out strategy that represents an important, positive step. However, responsibility for the pace of implementation falls squarely on the individual Pacific island countries themselves, rather than on any regional institutions or outside bodies.

Economic Growth

The Plan focuses on achieving faster, sustainable, pro-poor economic growth. This is to be achieved by means of greater trade, including in services; investment; improved efficiency and effectiveness in infrastructure and public service delivery; and increased private sector participation in, and contribution to, development. The main regional initiatives continue to be PICTA, PACER, and the forthcoming Economic Partnership Agreement (EPA) with the European Union.[2] It is proposed to integrate into PICTA both trade in services and the movement of Pacific island labor to more advanced economies for seasonal work, although the latter has not been endorsed by Australia and New Zealand. Another initiative is the Regional Trade Facilitation Program (RTFP), which seeks to standardize import taxes, customs regulations, and animal and plant hygiene and quarantine requirements. This will mean stronger competitive pressures among countries, but will also allow for economies of scale and create more jobs. In due course, a regional tourism marketing and investment plan is to be set up. Improved regional transport services are also envisaged, including development of the Pacific Aviation Safety Office, franchising of shipping services, and integrated development of ports.

Pacific Forum Economic Ministers have long recognized the importance of the private sector as a contributor to economic growth (see also Chapter 3). Discussions at their annual meetings have focused on the need for a more favorable climate for investment (including foreign direct investment), the benefits of policy consultation with the private sector, public-private partnerships, and the impact of trade arrangements, taxation regimes, land issues, and country risk. One of the background papers for the Plan addressed the high costs of doing business in the Pacific and discussed such bottlenecks as delays in obtaining approval to start a business; complicated procedures for hiring and firing workers; insufficient access to credit; uncertainties regarding enforcement of legal contracts; and cumbersome procedures for closing a business, particularly bankruptcy laws that can take years to apply.

The Plan incorporates the recommendations of another background paper on principles for the governance and management of public enterprises, which outlines ways to improve their efficiency, effectiveness, and financial sustainability. The Plan calls for preparation in each country of a coherent policy toward state enterprises, incorporating adherence to

---

[2]In June 2002, EU foreign ministers adopted a mandate for the European Commission to negotiate EPAs with Africa, the Caribbean, and the Pacific (ACP). There are four pillars to the EPAs: (1) partnership—the EU is to open up its market and eliminate trade barriers, and the ACP states are to strengthen supply capacity and reduce transaction costs; (2) regional integration—EPAs are to be based on regional integration initiatives; (3) development—EPAs will take account of the economic, social, and environmental constraints of the ACP countries; (4) link to the World Trade Organization (WTO)—EPAs will define bilateral and operational trade-related provisions within the broad framework of WTO rules. The three EPAs are scheduled to go into effect by January 2008. (Source: http://europa.eu.int/comm/trade/issues/bilateral/regions/acp/nepa_en.htm)

good corporate governance, and including rules and responsibilities for shareholders, boards, and management. Community service obligations are to be regularly examined and separated from commercial operations and transparently funded by governments. Both financial performance and service quality are to be monitored against appropriate national and international benchmarks. The Plan neither explicitly outlines a strategy for privatization nor defines its potential scope in the region.

Sustainable Development

The Plan encourages each country to develop and implement a National Sustainable Development strategy. Reflecting the regional approach of the Plan, these strategies are meant to incorporate regional conservation and management measures for the sustainable utilization of fisheries resources; regional plans for waste management; and a Pacific Islands Energy Policy to provide reliable, affordable, and environmentally sound energy for sustainable development. Proposals for dealing with Pacific climate change and reducing disaster relief and management include greater public awareness, capacity building, and strengthened governance, risk, and vulnerability assessment. Harmonized approaches in the health sector are expected to address HIV/AIDS and noncommunicable diseases through improved training, enhanced facilities to promote primary health care and immunization, and improved child and maternal health.

Good Governance

Good governance is defined as the transparent, accountable, and equitable management of all resources. The Plan considers good governance a prerequisite for economic growth and sustainable development. It endorses commitments to establish regional audit, ombudsman, and human rights offices to support integrity and oversight. Anticorruption institutions are envisaged, with associated legislation and performance guidance for national attorneys general, including through judicial training and education. Enhanced governance mechanisms for resource management are to be initiated with due regard for the need to harmonize traditional and modern cultural values and structures. This would apply to strengthening traditional courts; improving parliamentary effectiveness; training for peace building and conflict resolution; and developing new models for land ownership, tenure, and use. There would be technical assistance to strengthen treasury and finance functions and to augment country and regional statistical information services and databases.

Security

Security is defined as the stable and safe social and political conditions that are necessary for and reflective of good governance and sustainable development and for the achievement of faster economic growth. The Plan proposes the development and implementation of strategies and associated legislation for maritime and aviation security and surveillance; regional cooperation in border security, including for fighting transnational crime; mentoring for national financial intelligence units; information sharing among law enforcement agencies; and upgrading intelligence services. The regional law enforcement training courses would cover customs; immigration; family, domestic, gender, and sexual violence; human rights; juvenile justice; drug control; exclusive economic zone patrol programs; and military police. Plans for mitigation and management of natural disasters are to be prepared.

Monitoring and Evaluation

Implementation of the Plan will be measured by monitoring and evaluation of its initiatives, although it is agreed that a regional approach will be taken up only if it adds value to national efforts. Indicators have been developed to suit the regional context, as well as to allow for measurement of nationally and globally agreed targets, such as the Millennium Development Goals (MDGs). Political oversight and guidance to the Forum Secretariat will be provided by the Pacific Plan Action Committee, chaired by the Forum and comprising representatives of all Pacific island countries, perhaps at the cabinet level. Additionally, an independent comprehensive review of progress will be conducted every three years.

Indicators for monitoring progress in economic growth include annual percentage increases in the volume and value of goods and services traded by each country, tourist arrivals for each country, GDP per capita, foreign direct investment inflows for each country, the number of registered and operating businesses, and employment in the private sector. Measurement could also be made of annual percentage reductions in the number of canceled flights to and from trading partners and the relative costs of port and transport services for shipping a container to and from trading partners.

Indicators for monitoring progress in development include reductions in the number of people living in poverty, disaggregated into urban and rural sectors; the depth of poverty, defined as the difference between the poverty line and the average income of those who live below that line; the youth unemployment rate; and maternal mortality rates and mortality rates for children under age five. Measurement would also be needed for annual increases in sustainable access to potable water, sanitation, waste collection and disposal, and electricity—all in terms of the percentage of the total population and for both urban and rural areas.

Indicators for good governance include a voice and accountability measure designed to assess political, civil, and human rights; a political stability measure to determine the likelihood of violent threats to, or changes in, government, including terrorism; a government effectiveness measure to review the competence of the bureaucracy and the quality of public service; a regulatory measure for the incidence of market-unfriendly policies; a rule-of-law measure to gauge the quality of contract enforcement, the police, and the courts as well as the likelihood of crime and corruption; and a measure to show progress in the control of corruption. On security, indicators include country evaluations by the Financial Action Task Force of the Asia Pacific Group on Money Laundering, percentage reductions in crime against persons, and the average time taken to respond to national disasters in the region.

Final Comments

The Plan depends on support for regional approaches by Pacific island countries, civil society and private sector organizations, development partners, and other stakeholders. The type of regionalism that will best benefit the region is one that addresses capacity constraints and the lack of economic opportunities, as outlined in the Plan. Large public sectors, governance issues, corruption, and failure to promote the private sector have contributed to poor economic performance in recent years. The objectives of the Plan address these problems.

The Plan does not assess monetary and exchange rate policies, where the record in the region has generally been good. There have been questions from time to time about the need for such small states to have central banks, but the policies of these institutions have been useful in helping to maintain macroeconomic stability and protecting the balance of payments and official external reserves. The IMF has consistently taken the view that the choice of exchange rate regime is the prerogative of individual countries, and it advises on policies that are consistent with those choices, whether they be a peg to a basket of currencies, dollarization, or floating. Recently, there has been increasing interest in a possible currency union in the region, but such a change does not appear appropriate at present (see Chapter 7).

5

Remittances and Migration

Christopher Browne

Remittances to developing countries have grown steadily over the past three decades. In many countries, they now constitute the largest single source of foreign exchange, ahead of export receipts and foreign direct investment. Firm data on remittances are difficult to obtain (Kiribati is an exception), but net private transfers in the balance of payments statistics may give a partial indication of the magnitude of flows. Experience in the Pacific region has been varied (Table 5.1). A number of countries in the region have very large receipts by developing country standards (Figure 5.1). Both Tonga, with remittances equivalent to 24 percent of GDP, and Samoa, with remittances of about 20 percent of GDP, have very large receipts by overall developing country standards, a result of the fact that a large proportion of their citizens are permanent residents of Australia, New Zealand, and the United States. Kiribati, with remittances of 18 percent of GDP, also has large receipts, mainly from earnings by seamen on foreign ships who have attended the local Marine Training Institute, which was established with donor aid in the 1970s.

Remittances are also useful sources of foreign exchange in several other Pacific island countries. Fiji obtains such inflows primarily from citizens of Indian origin who have become permanent residents abroad, notably in Australia and Canada, following military coups, the most recent of which occurred in 2000. Marshall Islands, Micronesia, and to a lesser extent Palau, receive remittances from the United States. Emigration from these countries to the United States has increased over at least the past decade because progressive declines in grant assistance have reduced public sector

Table 5.1. Selected Pacific Island Countries: Private Transfers and Worker Remittances
(In millions of U.S. dollars)

	2000	2001	2002	2003	2004
Fiji (personal remittances)	43.7	82.6	97.4	122.4	171.4
Kiribati (worker remittances)	6.1	5.7	6.0	11.3	14.0
Marshall Islands (net private transfers)[1]	−6.2	−6.2	−12.1	−12.2	−11.7
Micronesia (net private transfers)[1]	2.3	2.3	2.3	2.4	2.4
Palau (net private transfers)[1]	3.3	−1.4	−1.4	−1.3	−1.7
Samoa (net private transfers)	43.2	50.6	57.9	74.0	66.6
Tonga (net private transfers)[1]	45.3	52.9	58.8	79.7	81.1

Sources: IMF staff estimates and country data.
[1]Data for fiscal years ending June 30 for Tonga and September 30 for Marshall Islands, Micronesia, and Palau.

employment and because citizens of these countries need only a valid passport and no visa to work in the United States. However, in Marshall Islands, inflows are offset by nuclear compensation payments to land owners who live abroad and in Palau, by payments to Asian employees in the construction and tourism sectors. The Melanesian countries of Papua New Guinea, Solomon Islands, and Vanuatu receive virtually no remittances, as there has been no tradition of emigration in modern times.

Future Remittance Flows

Remittances in the region are expected to stay at their present scale over the medium term, but a continuing flow of new migrants will be necessary to ensure continued remittance flows. This should be possible because of the well-established links with traditional destination countries such as Australia, New Zealand, and the United States, although it is unlikely that any major new channels will open. Furthermore, with job shortages expected to continue in the region, there should be plenty of people willing to seek better opportunities abroad, even if faster rates of sustainable economic growth are achieved. Their ability to find jobs is enhanced when they have relations, friends, and local communities in the recipient country, which is common.

At present, however, there is little labor mobility within the Pacific region, in part because many countries have legislation and regulations favoring their own citizens for job openings in the formal sector, a reflection of the high level of unemployment. Efforts to expand labor mobility will likely enhance remittance flows. The regional integration embodied

Figure 5.1. Fifteen Largest Development Countries Recipients of Remittances as Share of GDP
(1990–2003 average)

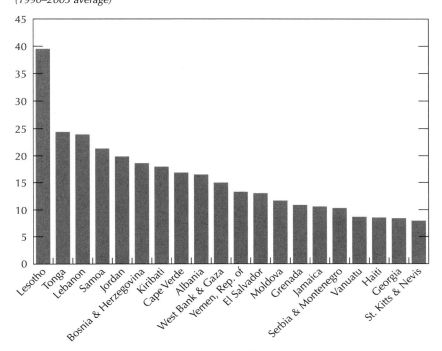

Source: IMF, *World Economic Outlook,* April 2005, Chapter II.

in the Pacific Plan provides for further examination of Pacific labor market issues, including greater mobility throughout the region and beyond. One of the stated long-term objectives of PICTA is the creation of a single market in the region, which would at some point extend to the movement of capital and labor.

Uses of Remittances

Remittances play a critical role in reducing the vulnerability of individuals in recipient countries to economic downturns or natural calamities. In the Pacific, they are primarily spent by families to maintain or increase expenditure on consumption needs, housing, education, health care, and small business activities. The last may include, in the agricultural sector, purchases of seeds, fertilizer, and tools to produce food to market. Business

investments are often focused on the purchases of shops and the establishment of taxi and other transport businesses. Other uses include church
donations, weddings, funerals, and local development projects. Because of
social structures and customs, Pacific islanders have a high propensity both
to remit and to do so longer than migrants from other regions. Samoans
and Tongans living abroad, in particular, maintain very strong ties with
their families, villages, and churches, and this is true even among second-
and third-generation migrants.

Remittances provide an important source of funds at most income levels. Emigrants' motivations for sending contributions tend to evolve over
their careers, and three phases are frequently identified. At first, the contributions appear to be essentially for families to meet basic consumption
needs, but they may later expand to include telephones, sound systems,
computers, and outboard motors. There is progressively greater emphasis
on human capital investment for the next generation, including support
for schooling in the home country and later possibly for tertiary study
abroad. Finally, the focus moves to investments to meet future retirement
needs if migrants plan to return home, including for living expenses, business investments, and real estate purchases.

The Impact of Remittances and Migration

The overall impact of remittances on fostering economic growth is hard
to determine and has not been effectively measured in the Pacific region,
although it is generally agreed that the impact is positive. Studies show
that households with access to remittances provide their children with
more education and better health care, engage in small business formation
on a greater scale, and accumulate more assets. There is also a close link
between remittances and poverty reduction, if the additional resources
are used for basic consumption. However, more comprehensive data are
needed on the sources and size of remittances, supplemented by greater
use of household surveys, if there are to be more accurate measures of the
effect on growth and poverty reduction. Efforts should also be made to
assess informal flows. A very substantial amount of cash and goods, primarily imported food and household items, is sent informally with people
traveling home to the Pacific islands, especially during the Christmas
season. In return, emigrants are often given goods to take back with them,
usually local food and handicrafts, which are not recorded as exports.

One worrisome aspect of emigration is the potential for a permanent
loss of skilled labor from the Pacific, especially of youth and the well-

educated. There is no doubt that emigrants tend to have higher skill levels than the general population. Even though emigrants may find better work opportunities and may gain experience that will prove valuable if they repatriate, the loss of human capital may hamper the development process, particularly because skills are already in such short supply in the region. Furthermore, the population loss may reduce government service delivery, because of erosion of the tax base, and increase property prices, which may make it even more difficult for those left behind to abandon subsistence agriculture.

There may have been some shift in recent years of remittance flows from informal channels to formal banking arrangements, reflecting a general easing of exchange rate restrictions and increased regulation, especially in the wake of the terrorist attacks of September 11, 2001. When remittances are deposited with financial institutions, a larger share of the population can come into contact with the formal financial system, expanding the cash economy, especially in rural areas, and promoting development. This facilitates the encouragement of savings accounts, the greater availability of credit, and the provision of education loans, home mortgages, and borrowing for the establishment of small businesses. It is generally agreed that policies should be developed to promote the sending of remittances through official channels, thereby encouraging migrants to save in financial assets at home and not abroad.

Governments must ensure that policies do not discourage remittance inflows. One concern is that remittances can be used to launder money and finance terrorism, and remittance service providers must be appropriately regulated to reduce this risk. However, supervisory frameworks must take into account, and where possible minimize, any adverse impact on the costs of sending remittances. There should also be no attempt to tax remittances, which are always derived from privately earned sources of income and may well have been taxed in the countries where emigrants are employed. Finally, no government steps should be taken to direct remittances, which will remain privately owned by local citizens, to specific sectors and purposes.

6

The Pacific Islands and the Eastern Caribbean Currency Union: A Comparative Review

Claims that similarities among small island developing countries call for the implementation of similar development strategies and underlying economic policies need to be nuanced. Despite their basic similarities, there can be substantial structural differences among island economies in different parts of the world and at different stages of economic development. Proper consideration of these differences is essential for the design of appropriate economic policies aimed at reaching stable and sustainable economic and social development.

This chapter examines and compares structural traits and macroeconomic developments and policies in the Pacific island countries and the Eastern Caribbean Currency Union (ECCU) countries over 1995–2004.[1] At the start of this 10-year period, the ECCU countries had reached a more advanced stage of development and had experienced more economic

---

[1]For this chapter, the Pacific islands group excludes Papua New Guinea, which would bias the analysis because of its large size relative to the other countries included in the comparison. In addition, only ECCU countries that are members of the IMF are included: Antigua and Barbuda, Dominica, Grenada, St. Kitts and Nevis, St. Lucia, and St. Vincent and the Grenadines; Anguilla and Montserrat, two territories of the United Kingdom that are also members of the ECCU, are excluded.

42

success than the Pacific island countries. Keeping in mind the structural differences among the countries in these two groups, this study tries to identify lessons to be learned and mistakes to be avoided from the ECCU experiences that could help the Pacific island countries in their pursuit of higher and more stable economic growth.

The following section provides a comparative description of the two groups of countries, highlighting similarities and differences based first on geography and climate and second on history, culture, and institutional heritage. The subsequent section compares macroeconomic developments and underlying economic policies over the last 10 years, with a focus on most recent developments. The concluding section explores the challenges ahead for the Pacific island countries and summarizes the lessons to be learned from the experiences of the ECCU countries.

A Comparative Description

Geography and Climate

Both these country groups consist of small tropical islands, but, with closer scrutiny, their geography proves to be rather different. Countries in both groups have a tropical climate and are similarly subject to hurricanes and their often devastating consequences. Both groups include a few volcanic islands, which adds eruptions and earthquakes to the list of natural disasters that can hit their people and cause huge shocks to their economies. Nonetheless, some finer geographic differences and the diverse location of the two country groups help explain their unequal economic performance and potential.

Most Pacific island countries are archipelagos made up of a few small islands and numerous islets scattered in a vast and remote area of the South Pacific Ocean. The average country covers a larger and more dispersed land territory than the average ECCU country and exercises control over an extended, exclusive economic zone. Distances among Pacific island countries are very large on average, limiting the incentives and reducing the opportunities for closer economic and political relations. On average, population is larger in the Pacific island countries, but the density is much lower.

ECCU countries are composed mainly of individual islands of limited size, concentrated in a small portion of the North Atlantic, relatively close to both the United States and the South American continent. Small distances among them and proximity to large and advanced external markets have facilitated the emergence of deepening economic and political ties. Average population is small, but density is relatively high.

History, Culture, and Institutional Heritage

Pacific and Caribbean island countries share a similar colonial background, but the colonial legacy and resulting cultural homogeneity are much stronger in the ECCU countries. The United Kingdom was the main colonial power in all ECCU countries and in several Pacific island countries; most of them gained independence only in the 1970s and 1980s. The British had greater strategic interests and therefore a longer and stronger administrative presence in the Caribbean, which left the British legal and institutional inheritance more deeply embedded in the administrative and political systems of ECCU countries. In the Pacific island countries, the institutional legacy has been weaker.

Caribbean island countries share the same ethnic and cultural background, which is anchored in a mixture of African and European heritage that, over time, developed into distinctive forms of Caribbean cultural expression, including music and cuisine. English is the official language in all ECCU countries, and all are members of the British Commonwealth of Nations. Their legal systems are based on common law and are subject to the supervisory jurisdiction of the Eastern Caribbean Supreme Court. Political and social stability have been common features of ECCU countries. This stability, along with their shared background, has been essential in promoting deep economic integration in the region, of which the currency union is but one tangible sign.

In contrast, cultural diversity in the Pacific islands is wide and is often the cause of political instability. Micronesian, Melanesian, and Polynesian cultures intermix in these countries, and often within different communities within a single country. Numerous languages are spoken, even among members of the same ethnic group. English is generally one of two or more official languages in each country, and it is often spoken in pidgin form. All the countries in the region are members of the British Commonwealth except the three former U.S.-administered United Nations Trust Territories—Marshall Islands, Micronesia, and Palau. The legal systems in all countries are based on common law tradition but are complemented with local customs. Political instability has been occasionally evident, culminating in civil war as in Solomon Islands during 1999–2003, or with the temporary abandonment of democratic government for military rule as in Fiji, most recently in 2000. (Table 6.1 summarizes the geographical and institutional characteristics of countries in these two regions.)

Table 6.1. Pacific Island and ECCU Countries: Geography and Institutional Inheritance

	Population (Thousands)	Area (Thousands of square km.)	Density (Population per square km.)	Year of Independence
Pacific Island Countries				
Fiji	840	18.3	48	1970
Kiribati	90	0.7	138	1971
Marshall Islands	58	0.2	318	1986
Micronesia	108	0.7	154	1986
Palau	20	0.5	44	1994
Samoa	181	2.8	64	1962
Solomon Islands	470	28.0	19	1978
Tonga	101	0.7	153	1970
Vanuatu	215	12.2	17	1980
Total	2,185	64.1	34	. . .
Average	243	7.1	106	1977
Eastern Caribbean Currency Union Countries				
Antigua and Barbuda	71	0.4	162	1981
Dominica	72	0.8	96	1978
Grenada	104	0.3	306	1974
St. Kitts and Nevis	42	0.4	116	1983
St. Lucia	177	0.6	290	1979
St. Vincent and the Grenadines	107	0.4	273	1979
Total	572	2.9	198	. . .
Average	95	0.5	207	1979

Sources: World Bank, 2005 World Development Indicators; IMF, World Economic Outlook database; and CARICOM Website.

Macroeconomic Performance and Policies

Geographic, historic, and cultural homogeneity in the Caribbean is mirrored by strongly correlated economic performance and stable macroeconomic indicators. Growth volatility over time and across countries has been limited in the ECCU group, and fluctuations in domestic output have been shown to be strongly correlated with business cycle fluctuations in industrial countries. Economic performance in the Pacific has instead been subject to high volatility and large cross-country variability. Numerous empirical studies of developing country economies have found that high volatility in economic growth is generally associated with lower growth levels, and the growth experiences of countries in these two regions over the last 10 years support this conclusion.

Positive growth and stable macroeconomic management between 1995 and 2004 underpinned higher and rising living standards in ECCU coun-

Table 6.2. Pacific Island and ECCU Countries: Selected Macroeconomic Indicators

	Pacific Island Countries	Eastern Caribbean Currency Union Countries
GDP in millions of US$ (2004)		
Total	4,335	3,092
Average	482	515
Real GDP growth (percent)		
Average		
1995–2004	1.7	2.6
2002–04	1.6	2.1
Inflation (percent)		
Average		
1995–2004	3.7	1.8
2002–04	4.1	1.4
Current account balance in percent of GDP (2002–04)		
Average	–0.6	–20.3

Sources: IMF, World Economic Outlook database; and IMF staff estimates.

tries (Table 6.2). Average per capita income in U.S. dollars increased by a cumulative 50 percent, reaching US$6,188 in 2004. The equivalent indicator in the Pacific region stood at about US$2,300 in 2004, reflecting average cumulative growth of 39 percent over the same period. Even the worst-performing member of the ECCU experienced positive growth in annual per capita income (2.5 percent on average); the worst performer among the Pacific island countries recorded a cumulative decline in per capita income of almost 20 percent. However, a 1996 study comparing developments in these two regions found that official statistics tend to underestimate the size of subsistence sector activities, which is an important share of GDP in the Pacific and is irrelevant in the Caribbean. A correction on that account would imply a marginal increase of per capita GDP in the Pacific and only minor reductions in cross-country variability.

Of course, diverging trends in living standards in the two country groups also reflect differences in demographics. Whereas in ECCU countries population grew at a moderate annual average rate of 0.4 percent during 1995–2004, annual population growth in the Pacific island countries averaged 1.7 percent over the same period. Slower population growth reflects and probably reinforces the remarkable social and economic progress achieved by the small Caribbean islands since independence.

The sectoral composition of the two regions' economies is rather different. The Caribbean economies are heavily skewed toward services—

particularly tourism—and on average include rather small agriculture sectors. Conversely, agriculture still accounts for a significant share of domestic value added in the Pacific island countries' GDP, including a nontrivial (though declining) share of low-productivity subsistence agriculture. More recently, however, the share of services—tourism-related services in particular—has been growing fast in several Pacific countries. This reflects both growing demand from Australia and New Zealand, currently the main markets for tourism services in the South Pacific, and a stronger focus on policies in support of tourism by policymakers in the region. Growing tourism activity and related investment have contributed substantially to the recent acceleration of growth.

Inflation

Over the last 10 years, average inflation has been relatively tame in both regions (see Table 6.2). Supported by the currency union and peg to the U.S. dollar, ECCU countries' average inflation remained below 2 percent during 1995–2004, and declined to 1.4 percent during 2002–04. Favorable access to external financing and relatively developed financial systems have allowed the Eastern Caribbean Central Bank to keep inflation at these low levels, despite persistent and large fiscal deficits in most ECCU countries.

Average inflation in the Pacific during 1995–2004 was moderate at 3.7 percent, notwithstanding higher exchange rate flexibility. Limited correlation between real and monetary developments in the region explains the large cross-country variability in inflation. More recently, inflation in the Pacific has been on the rise, reaching a cross-country average of 4.1 percent during 2002–04. This reflects a rapid expansion in domestic credit in response to growing economic activity in the largest countries in the region. To keep further inflationary pressures at bay, central banks in the concerned countries will need to closely monitor credit aggregates and, if warranted, use monetary policy operations to rein in excessive credit expansion.

Capital Account and Fiscal Balances

There have been diverging developments in the capital account balances of countries in these two regions, reflecting, on the one hand, high levels of grant assistance to the Pacific and, on the other hand, high foreign direct investment (FDI) and debt financing in the Caribbean. Persistent and large deficits have been the norm among ECCU countries over the entire 10-year period under examination. In recent years, the average current account deficit has widened to about 20 percent of GDP. Large FDI flows, reflecting positive growth prospects and a stable currency, have been the main source of financing for these current account deficits, but debt financing for public investment has been rising rapidly. Moreover, to offset sharp declines in official development assistance, there has been increasing use of commercial borrowing. The solid credibility of the currency regime, stable growth, and relatively developed financial systems have granted ECCU countries access to international commercial lending to finance expansionary fiscal policies.

Large levels of per capita aid have helped keep the Pacific island countries' external positions at manageable levels, despite limited FDI inflows and constrained access to commercial borrowing. Though external financing constraints may have reduced growth opportunities, more moderate and declining levels of external debt now leave these countries in a stronger position to face future shocks.

On average, Pacific countries recorded stronger fiscal balances than ECCU countries over 1995–2004, but high variability across the region reflects substantial differences in fiscal structures and policy stances. Limited access to external borrowing and few possibilities for noninflationary domestic financing have restricted the set of fiscal options available to Pacific governments. Average ratios of expenditure and revenue to GDP have been higher in the Pacific, which largely reflects very high spending and large external assistance flows to the smaller countries. Among the larger Pacific countries, spending and revenue levels are closer to those in the Caribbean. However, ECCU countries have run larger fiscal deficits on average. Access to external commercial borrowing and a more developed domestic financial system—including a regional government securities market for the issuance and secondary market trading of government securities—explain the relative ease with which governments have been able to finance growing fiscal deficits. Yet four of six of these countries now have total public debt levels well above 100 percent of GDP, and so fiscal consolidation is now an urgent need. In the Pacific, there are lower public debt levels, most of which are on a downward trend, and this leaves most countries with manageable fiscal positions.

Trade and Tariffs

There is a trend in both regions toward increasing trade liberalization, and so the revenue contribution of trade taxes is expected to decline.

Table 6.3. Pacific Island and ECCU Countries: Per Capita Aid (US$)

	Pacific Island Countries	Eastern Caribbean Currency Union Countries
Average	476	80
Maximum	1,295	153
Minimum	61	0

Source: World Bank, 2005 World Development Indicators.

Governments need to plan ahead for alternative tax policy measures to off-set expected revenue losses from trade taxes. In line with their membership in the Caribbean Community and Common Market (CARICOM), ECCU countries have largely harmonized their trade regimes, and trade in goods is already practically free among them. As part of the integration process, these countries have adopted a common external tariff (CET). Originally, the plan was for the CET to be gradually reduced in four stages from 1993 to 1998, with the maximum tariff rate declining from 35 to 20 percent. Based on revenue concerns, a few ECCU countries have yet to implement the final stage of tariff reductions, exposing their lack of effective tax policy instruments to offset revenue losses from trade liberalization.

Regional integration in the Pacific is still at a very early stage, but most countries will need to compensate for the revenue losses that will eventually result from trade liberalization. Tariff levels and structures now vary substantially among these countries, as do their general tax regimes.

Development Assistance

Development assistance to ECCU countries has been declining, but substantial aid flows continued to the Pacific over 1995–2004 (Table 6.3). During the 1980s, ECCU countries were large recipients of international aid, which they used to finance important public investment programs, particularly in infrastructures. With these countries moving up on the development ladder, donors gradually reduced their support, which has more recently consisted mainly of assistance for natural disaster relief.

Concessional development assistance to the Pacific has remained strong, especially from regional bilateral donors (mainly Australia and New Zealand) and from the United States for the three Compact countries (Marshall Islands, Micronesia, and Palau). In fact, the Pacific island countries, particularly the smaller ones, are among the largest recipients of international aid in per capita terms. However, generous assistance has not yet succeeded in leading most of these countries to the path of stable, self-sustainable growth.

This is particularly true for the Compact countries, which will remain heavily dependent on grants from the United States for several years to come. Within a context of revived pledges by donors to support economic development, several donors—mainly from the region—have committed to increase the size and strengthen the effectiveness of their assistance to the Pacific island countries. Most recently, Australia and New Zealand have started framing their assistance programs in the region in the context of long-term engagement plans. Finally, donor coordination is being strengthened and is increasingly focused on building the institutions and physical and human capital deemed essential for establishing the conditions for private-sector-led growth.

Public Spending

The ratio of government spending to GDP has been high in both regions, at 36 percent of GDP in the ECCU and 42 percent of GDP in the Pacific, on average, over 2002–04. The long-term trend seems more encouraging in the Pacific, where government spending in GDP terms has been declining, although public spending levels in the smaller Pacific countries remain well above the average for developing countries. Given the relatively low growth achieved over the same period in both regions, high public spending appears to have been ineffective at promoting higher levels of economic activity.

The wage bill is generally the largest expenditure component in both regions, amounting on average to 13 percent in the Caribbean and close to 16 percent in the Pacific (with high variation between the smaller and larger countries). In a recent regional study, the World Bank estimated that, in 2002, government employment in the ECCU countries absorbed an average of 20 percent of the labor force and that government wages over 1995–2002 grew faster than real per capita incomes. Comparable data for the Pacific island countries are not available, but the higher ratios of total wages to GDP suggest that public employment must account for an important share of formal employment. Policymakers in the region claim that small size and great territorial dispersion justify larger numbers of public employees to provide basic public services to poorer citizens in remote and isolated villages. Questioning the validity of such an argument, however, is anecdotal evidence that suggests that public employment is concentrated in urban areas.

Development expenditure has, on average, constituted a low share of public spending in the Pacific and has often borne the brunt of fiscal adjustment efforts in the region. ECCU governments, instead, have dedicated a large share of their spending to public investment, particularly during the 1980s, when external assistance was abundant. In the late

1990s and early 2000s, these countries raised public spending, including for investment, trying to offset exogenous shocks on growth and declining private investment. The fiscal expansions did not translate into a revival of growth and instead resulted in the buildup of debt.

Governments in both regions have more recently come to grips with the failure of high government spending to stimulate growth and have started to explore policy options to reduce the incidence of government spending in the economy and make space for more private-sector-led economic activity and employment. They have now accepted that a sustainable fiscal correction needs to include downward revisions to the wage bill and a leaner and more effective civil service.

Lessons for the Pacific from the ECCU Experience

The near-term challenges facing countries in the Pacific are different from those facing countries in the Caribbean, although the search for faster, stable growth is the leading preoccupation in both regions. In theory, the Pacific island countries should have experienced faster growth rates than the ECCU countries over the past 10 years, given their lower starting level of economic development (barring exogenous shocks). The fact that this did not happen suggests that policies in the Pacific countries, although effective at maintaining relative macroeconomic stability over 1995–2004, have not been effective at promoting growth. Clearly, while macroeconomic stability is a necessary condition for growth, it is not sufficient. Limited progress with structural reforms is the likely explanation for the region's sluggish long-term growth.

The Pacific island countries today are at a stage of economic development that the ECCU countries reached in the late 1980s. At that time, the Caribbean island countries were growing faster on account of strong public investment in infrastructure, which was largely funded through official development assistance and the adoption of policies in support of private-sector-led investment, particularly in tourism. Tourism was the engine for growth and diversification in these economies, and it remains a major source of employment and export earnings in the region, despite having now reached the stage of maturity, which entails somewhat lower growth dynamics.

Although tourism in the Caribbean benefits greatly from its proximity to the large North American market, the region also manages to attract significant numbers of European tourists. And proximity to a large market is no longer necessarily a limiting factor for the development of a successful

Table 6.4. Pacific Island and ECCU Countries: Tourism Growth
(Annual growth rate)

	Tourist arrivals		Tourism Receipts	
	1990–2000	2000–03	1990–2000	2000–03
ECCU Countries	3.6	1.9	3.0	1.6
Pacific Island Countries	2.7	8.2	2.7	5.0

Sources: World Tourism Organization and IMF staff estimates.

tourism sector. Witness the fast development of tourism in very isolated destinations such as Mauritius or Maldives that have become very fashionable worldwide. In recent years, tourist arrivals and overall receipts from tourist spending have been growing fast in several Pacific island countries (Table 6.4). Larger foreign investment and successful efforts by policymakers to adopt policies in support of tourism have helped build capacity to respond to increasing demand. However, progress has been slow in leveraging tourism growth to create significant demand spillovers in other sectors in the domestic economy. Advances on this front will mostly depend on the effectiveness of policymakers in improving the legal and regulatory environment for private investment to reduce the cost of doing business in their countries.

Private investment has been limited in the Pacific region by the legal and regulatory framework, the business environment, and the quality of infrastructure. Land ownership issues are of specific concern in the Pacific islands, with no parallel in the Caribbean. The Pacific system of customary land ownership entails problems for land development and presents challenges to investors that want to secure loans against property. Several Pacific island countries are currently reviewing their system of land rights with the objective of accommodating the customary system of land ownership while at the same time permitting the use of land as collateral by giving more certainty to long-term land-lease titles. In addition to problems of land ownership, the general business environment in the Pacific significantly inflates the costs of doing business. High costs are partly explained by these economies' isolation and small size, but they are compounded by the existence of badly regulated, often state-owned, inefficient monopolies that provide essential services for business operations, such as power, telecommunications, and transportation services.

The recent reform of the telecommunication sector in ECCU countries provides an encouraging example of how regional cooperation among small island countries can support private sector development. The establishment in 2000 of the Eastern Caribbean Telecommunications Authority

(ECTEL)—the regional regulator for telecommunications—has accompanied the dismantling of subregional monopolies and the introduction of competition into the markets for fixed and mobile telecommunications. Costs have declined significantly, and the number of firms and employees now operating in the sector has doubled.

In the Pacific, the discouraging effects on private investment of high-cost, low-quality utilities are aggravated by poor infrastructure. The region's governments, together with donors, need to strengthen public investment efforts and ensure that such programs focus on developing physical and human capital that complement rather than substitute for private sector investment. As in ECCU countries, policymakers in the Pacific have increasingly used fiscal incentives to promote private investment, particularly foreign direct investment. The ECCU's long experience with investment incentives suggests that the effectiveness of such policies in promoting new investment and growth has been limited. In particular, while still high, investment flows in ECCU countries have not kept pace with the rest of the Caribbean or in the world at large. Fiscal incentives have been very costly in terms of forgone revenue and have created perverse incentive-based competition among ECCU countries. Given the similarity of ECCU countries, investors are to a large degree indifferent about where exactly to locate their operations. Hence, incentive-based competition among potential host countries has meant that a larger part of the gains from new investment accrues to the investor rather than to the eventual host country. Extensive use of tax incentives and administrative exemptions have also created complex and nontransparent tax systems, creating fertile ground for the emergence of governance issues.

Pacific island countries should review their existing systems of tax incentives and design a strategy aimed at establishing business-friendly, nondiscriminatory tax systems across the region. Regional coordination in this task could be beneficial. Simpler and more transparent tax regimes are also easier to administer, which is an important quality, particularly for the smaller Pacific countries, where tax and customs administration already suffers from limited skills availability.

A unified monetary regime on the model of the ECCU is not a short-term option for the Pacific island countries. The decision by the ECCU to establish a single central bank in the early 1980s was natural—those countries had been using the same currency practically since 1950, under their colonial ruler (the United Kingdom). The small size of each individual country, their proximity, strong similarities, openness, and links to the same external markets made the choice for a formal monetary union a simple one. The dollar-pegged currency union managed by the Eastern

Caribbean Central Bank has been a pillar for macroeconomic stability and for the development of a sound banking system. The currency union has failed, however, to promote adequate fiscal discipline in ECCU member countries. In fact, its strong credibility has even been a factor in relaxing the financial constraints on these countries, thus indirectly allowing for the buildup of excessive debt.

The Pacific island countries do not meet any of the conditions that would make monetary unification a sensible option or would bring benefits to their economies. On the other hand, the recent ECCU experience provides a strong warning that, should such a move be considered by the Pacific countries in the more distant future, monetary unification needs to be supported by clear and enforceable criteria for maintaining fiscal discipline among its members.

In their attempts at closer regional integration, the Pacific island countries can learn from the ECCU countries' experience. Again, strong similarities, proximity, and the small size of their individual economies motivated ECCU members and other countries in the larger Caribbean region to undertake an extensive process, still ongoing, of economic integration (through CARICOM). Regional trade integration in itself has not provided significant benefits to ECCU countries and has actually caused trade diversion in favor of imports from larger CARICOM members. However, deepening trade integration within the Caribbean region has created opportunities to move further as a group toward integration within wider regional markets such as the Free Trade Area of the Americas, which could provide more tangible benefits to ECCU countries through the planned liberalization of trade in services. Other regional initiatives, particularly for the provision of common services, such as ECTEL and the regional Directorate of Civil Aviation, have resulted in outright reductions in the costs of doing business and have shown that regional solutions can help depoliticize pricing issues in critical utility services.

The Pacific island governments need to begin implementing policies to effectively integrate their countries into the global economy. These countries can learn from the experiences of similar countries that are at a more advanced stage in this process, including by avoiding policies that have proven ineffective at promoting growth or have prevented the implementation of policies to adjust to global developments. To secure the real benefits from trade, economic integration among the Pacific island countries should become rapidly more oriented to wider trade integration rather than the creation of a small, subregional common market with strong external protection. Wider trade liberalization could be supported by regional initiatives in other areas that have proved helpful elsewhere, such as in the ECCU, in reducing the costs of doing business or the costs of government. Diversity among the Pacific island countries, including in terms of economic development and degree of dependence on external assistance, will mean that they require tailored policy advice for some time to come.

7

Options for Alternative Exchange Rate Arrangements

Susan Creane, Jun Il Kim, and Laura Papi, with assistance from Agnes Isnawangsih[1]

The question of what exchange rate regime best fits an individual economy continues to be much discussed by policymakers and academics. For the Pacific island countries, the question has particular resonance given the small size and openness of their economies and their resultant vulnerability to external shocks. However, there is no unambiguous answer, because an exchange rate system should be determined according to each country's macroeconomic and structural characteristics and economic, political, and institutional constraints. For that reason, the IMF supports the range of regimes chosen by individual countries in the region.

All the Pacific island countries have some form of pegged exchange rate regime, with the exception of Papua New Guinea, which has an independently floating exchange rate arrangement. According to the IMF official classification reported in the *Annual Report on Exchange Arrangements and Exchange Restrictions,* the currencies of Fiji, Samoa, and Vanuatu are pegged to a basket of currencies; the exchange rate regime of Solomon Islands is a crawling peg; and Tonga has a peg within horizontal bands. Other island countries are dollarized: Kiribati with the Australian dollar, and Marshall Islands, Micronesia, and Palau with the U.S. dollar. The

---

[1]This paper was presented at the December 2005 meeting of the South Pacific Central Bank Governors in response to their request for an analysis of the suitability of dollarization for the Pacific island countries.

analysis in this paper applies to the six countries that have their own currencies; it is assumed that those now dollarized will remain so.

This chapter discusses the pros and cons of a common currency union and the relative merits of a currency union that adopts the currency of another country (dollarization), most likely by using the Australian dollar. Then it outlines the theoretical criteria for establishment of a currency union and applies these criteria to the Pacific region using two different methods of empirical analysis. The chapter concludes with a discussion of some practical considerations related to forming a currency union in the Pacific island countries.

The Pros and Cons of a Currency Union

There are several potential advantages of a currency union over the maintenance by each country of an independent currency: lower inflation, to the extent that fiscal discipline is achieved; fiscal discipline, to the extent that the ability to finance budget deficits is limited or eliminated; and promotion of regional integration, to the extent that labor, capital, and goods are encouraged to move freely. These advantages, however, are realized only when supporting fiscal and structural policy actions are in place.

The main disadvantages for individual countries of a currency union are the loss of the exchange rate as a shock absorber, to the extent the fixed regime holds; the loss of independent monetary policy; the need for fiscal policy, prices, and wages to be sufficiently flexible; the loss of a lender-of-last-resort facility for individual countries; the loss of seigniorage, although some sharing arrangement can be devised within the union; and some loss of national sovereignty.

There are two possible types of currency unions: one that dollarizes or one with a common currency, either pegged to or floating against currencies outside the union. The potential advantages of dollarization or a common currency include more credibility, because the risk of devaluation is substantially reduced; less opportunity for inflationary financing, which can encourage investment; and closer integration with other countries that use the adopted currency, resulting in lower transaction costs and more stable prices. There are also some disadvantages to a common currency or dollarization, including that such an arrangement is much more difficult to reverse; large shocks, such as a sharp increase in world oil prices or a fall in the price of a key export, must be absorbed through nominal wages and domestic price adjustment; a much stronger and earlier level of political commitment is needed because most countries are reluctant to abandon their national currency; a loss of seigniorage, except in the unlikely case that the country whose currency is adopted agrees to share these revenues; and loss of the lender-of-last-resort role for individual central banks.

Do the Pacific Islands Meet the Criteria for an Effective Currency Union?

The benefits of adopting a currency union are greater when certain criteria are met. This section draws from the economic literature on optimum currency areas and fixed versus floating exchange rate regimes and applies the theoretical criteria for successful currency unions to the realities of the Pacific island region. Much of the analysis applies equally to currency unions with floating, pegged, or dollarized exchange rates and they are therefore differentiated only where relevant. In addition, some comparisons are made with the countries that comprise the ECCU, which are pegged to the U.S. dollar.

Trade Openness

Trade openness, a measure of a country's engagement in international trade, is calculated as the ratio of the sum of imports and exports to GDP. The importance of an economy's openness in determining its suitability for a currency union is ambiguous. On the one hand, the more open the economy, the larger the impact of external shocks, and therefore the more useful the exchange rate as an adjustment tool. On the other hand, the more open the economy and the more the countries in question trade with each other, the greater the potential reduction in transaction costs from a currency union. The outcome will depend in part on the extent to which nominal exchange rate changes translate into real exchange rate changes. If prices and wages adjust quickly with the exchange rate, the exchange rate is not an effective adjustment tool and the latter effect (a reduction in transactions costs) might dominate.

Trade openness is generally high in the Pacific island region, but it varies across countries and is lower than in the ECCU. For trade in goods and services, it ranges between 77 percent in Tonga and 118 percent in Fiji (Table 7.1). Openness has been broadly stable over the past decade, with the exception of Solomon Islands, where openness declined sharply as a result of civil strife and the resulting decline in economic activity and has not yet fully recovered.

Table 7.1. Pacific Island Countries: Direction of Trade
(In percent of total, period average unless otherwise indicated)

	Fiji	Papua New Guinea	Samoa	Solomon Islands	Tonga	Vanuatu	Average
Exports							
United States	24.5	1.7	8.2	1.6	33.0	3.0	12.0
Australia	20.6	26.9	64.3	2.1	1.4	2.3	19.6
New Zealand	3.6	1.0	1.7	0.4	4.5	0.5	2.0
Japan	4.8	8.5	1.5	16.2	40.9	10.3	13.7
Developing Asia	20.9	17.5	20.6	73.5	14.0	71.2	36.3
of which,							
other PICs	2.1	0.1	0.1	0.6	0.2	0.4	0.6
Rest of the world	30.4	52.9	5.2	22.3	47.1	22.9	30.1
Imports							
United States	2.5	2.4	14.4	3.4	8.6	1.7	5.5
Australia	36.7	48.0	16.1	27.8	10.8	18.1	26.2
New Zealand	17.1	4.9	19.7	5.8	34.1	7.2	14.8
Japan	4.2	4.1	10.0	3.6	4.8	16.3	7.2
Developing Asia	33.5	34.5	34.6	52.4	35.0	47.7	39.6
of which,							
other PICs	0.1	0.0	0.0	1.3	0.1	0.5	0.3
Rest of the world	10.2	10.3	15.2	10.6	11.5	25.3	13.9

Sources: IMF, World Economic Outlook and Direction of Trade Statistics databases.

Direction of Trade

Regional trade is minimal—no more than 2 percent of total trade for any country in the region, although PICTA aims to address this.

Australia is a major trading partner for the Pacific island countries. All countries, with the exception of Samoa, import more from Australia than they export to Australia. Imports from the United States are lower than from Australia. Trade with New Zealand is generally less than with Australia, although Samoa and Tonga have strong trade links. On average, trade with developing Asia is significant, with a large variation across countries for exports. The Pacific island countries seem less integrated with their major trading partner, Australia, than the ECCU countries are with the United States.[2]

Overall, limited trade within the region suggests that a currency union with a freely floating exchange rate would bring limited benefits to the Pacific island countries in terms of reduced transaction costs. But small,

---

[2]This remains true when trade is weighted according to the IMF Information Notice System, which takes into account third-country effects as well as the dominance of trading partners in commodity markets.

open economies often can reduce transaction costs by adopting the currency of a large trading partner. If the region were to consider adoption of another currency or a peg to another currency, the Australian dollar appears more suitable than the New Zealand dollar or the U.S. dollar. The origin of aid flows, remittances, and tourism receipts generally supports this conclusion.

Business Cycle Synchronization

The greater the co-movements in business cycles among countries in a currency union, the lower the cost of foregoing exchange rate flexibility and the greater the benefits from the currency union. When co-movements in business cycles are high, the policies of the anchor country in the currency union should also be supportive of economic stabilization in the other countries.

The anchor country for Pacific island countries would be Australia, and together their economies represent 0.2 percent of Australia's GDP. The United States is the anchor for the ECCU countries, which represent 0.008 percent of U.S. GDP. Among the Pacific island countries considered here, average economic growth correlations were a mere 7 percent in the past 10 years. Although average economic growth correlations with Australia have increased in the past decade, two countries had negative correlations with Australia. Even for the four countries with positive correlations, the degree of output correlations was on average only 18 percent, considerably less than the ECCU countries' average of 41 percent within their currency union or 43 percent with the United States. An analysis of output co-movements confirms the above findings.

Overall, the evidence suggests that Pacific island countries do not appear well suited for a currency union with a freely floating exchange rate nor for one that is either pegged to or adopts the Australian dollar, partly because synchronization of business cycles is either limited or nonexistent both within the region and between the region and Australia.

Terms of Trade

The smaller the size of terms of trade shocks and the higher the co-movements in the terms of trade for a group of countries, the greater the benefits of a currency union. Although their size has declined in the last 10 years, terms of trade shocks are still sizable in the Pacific island region (Table 7.2), and they are larger than those in the ECCU, indicating that the costs of

Table 7.2. Pacific Island Countries: Terms of Trade
(Averages of absolute annual changes)

	1985–94	1995–2004
Australia	6.73	4.13
Fiji	1.63	1.21
Pacific Islands	13.73	12.23
Papua New Guinea	6.35	8.72
Samoa	14.43	13.92
Solomon Islands	13.38	11.57
Tonga	21.20[1]	26.84
Vanuatu	25.41	11.14

Sources: IMF, *World Economic Outlook,* and IMF staff estimates.
[1] For Tonga is 1987–94.

giving up their national currencies would be higher for the Pacific countries. The terms of trade shocks are also considerably larger than in Australia. The co-movements of these countries' terms of trade with Australia vary widely, being negative for some and positive and large for others. Between pairs of different Pacific island countries, correlations also are highly variable, with some negative and others positive up to 60 percent.

Thus, the size and co-movements of the terms of trade indicate that, from this perspective, the region is not well suited for a common currency or for dollarization with the Australian dollar. Giving up the exchange rate as a tool for adjusting to terms of trade shocks would likely mean that adopting a currency union or dollarization would carry significant costs for these countries.

Natural disasters are another type of real shock that put a premium on maintaining the exchange rate as an adjustment tool. During the last five years most countries were subject to such shocks quite frequently, although the same disaster seldom affected more than one or two countries at the same time. This suggests that a common currency may not be desirable from this perspective.

Inflation

The higher and more variable the inflation rate and the higher the co-movements in prices, the greater the potential benefits of a pegged currency or dollarization. Inflation rates across the Pacific region were modest in the last 10 years and their variability was limited. The relative price stability in the Pacific island region does not indicate a strong need for a currency union either with a pegged currency or with dollarization to foster monetary stability.

Other Factors

Greater factor mobility can allow needed adjustment in the absence of exchange rate flexibility. Although data for this type of analysis are lacking, anecdotal evidence indicates that labor mobility in the region is limited. While the citizens of some countries have migrated outside the region in large numbers, this is not possible for others. Domestic labor markets also appear to have limited flexibility, especially because of large public sectors.

The greater the fiscal flexibility, the lower the costs of ceding exchange rate flexibility. A very rough indicator of such flexibility is the debt-to-GDP ratio, because the higher the debt level, the less room there is for using fiscal policy countercyclically. Fiscal flexibility differs by country in the region but in most cases is limited, given that public debt ranges from about 40 percent of GDP for Vanuatu to about 90 percent of GDP for Solomon Islands.

The lower the seigniorage, the smaller the cost of giving up the national currency. Rough calculations indicate that seigniorage in the region has averaged about 1 percent of GDP in recent years. As a notional comparison, the average seigniorage in the ECCU was ½ percent of GDP in the decade preceding their currency union.

Assessing the Region's Suitability for a Currency Union: An Index Approach

This section uses an index approach to analyze the region's suitability for a currency union or dollarization. The index combines various criteria for a currency union to measure the expected variability in bilateral exchange rates. A low value of the index denotes a high suitability for dollarization.

There are two different specifications for the index: one using nominal exchange rate variability as the dependent variable, and the other using an exchange market pressure variable, which is defined as a weighted change in bilateral nominal exchange rate and official reserves.[3] The latter may be more appropriate for countries using a fixed exchange rate regime. The

---

[3]A sample of 70 countries was used, including members of the European Monetary Union, other members of the Group of Seven industrialized nations, a selection of Asian-Pacific and Latin American countries, and the Pacific island countries. This approach is in line with the existing academic literature, with minor modifications to better suit developing countries.

regression analysis includes such explanatory variables as co-movements in output, prices, and the terms of trade, as well as trade openness and country size. Other variables that are discussed in the previous sections, such as indicators of labor market mobility and fiscal flexibility, either were not statistically significant or could not be included because of data constraints.

The findings are inconclusive about the region's suitability for a currency union with a floating exchange rate. Neither do they point to a clear suitability for dollarization, although they do indicate that the Pacific island countries may have become relatively more suited for dollarization over the past two decades, as the variability in their growth rates has declined. However, there is no indication that this trend will continue over the long term. The results also suggest that should dollarization be undertaken, use of the Australian dollar would be more advisable than use of the U.S. dollar. Fiji, Samoa, Solomon Islands, and Tonga are the countries most suitable for dollarization with the Australian dollar.

Alternative Exchange Rate Arrangements: Transitional Issues

Forming a currency union or dollarizing entails a range of operational issues. This section examines the experience of existing currency unions with a number of these issues and compares this experience with the current situation in the Pacific island region and Australia.

All currency unions have adopted convergence criteria on key variables to promote stable macroeconomic policies and minimize the potential costs imposed on others by nonperformers. Some convergence criteria are used as preconditions for membership and some apply after a country joins the union, with varying degrees of enforcement. Criteria typically include numerical targets on variables such as government deficits and debt, inflation, reserves, interest rates, and exchange rates.

The need for fiscal policy maneuverability is critical for the success of a currency union given the absence of other macroeconomic policy options. For this reason, fiscal convergence criteria figure prominently in transition and eligibility criteria for countries joining currency unions. The Pacific island region has made some progress toward improved fiscal conditions in recent years and most could now meet a typical fiscal balance criterion (Table 7.3). However, only two countries converge with the fiscal performance of Australia, which has been running consistent surpluses in recent years.

Table 7.3. Pacific Islands: Convergence Indicators

	Fiscal Balance/GDP					Government Debt/GDP					CPI					Lending Rates			
	2001	2002	2003	2004	2005	2001	2002	2003	2004	2005	2001	2002	2003	2004	2005	2001	2002	2003	2004
Fiji	−7	−6	−6	−5	−3	44	48	49	53	52	4	1	4	3	4	8.3	8.1	7.6	7.2
Papua New Guinea	−4	−6	−2	1	−1	62	73	70	57	51	9	12	15	2	2	16.2	13.9	13.4	13.3
Samoa	−2	−2	−2	−1	−1	61	59	53	50	48	4	8	4	2	2	9.9	9.8	9.8	9.8
Solomon Islands	−13	−11	−2	8	0	82	97	99	87	78	8	9	10	7	6	15.7	16.4	16.3	16.1
Tonga	−2	−1	−3	1	−1	68	72	69	62	53	7	10	11	12	11	11.3	11.4	11.3	11.6
Vanuatu	−4	−4	−2	1	0	38	41	41	38	37	4	2	3	1	2	8.8	7.4	5.9	7.6
Australia	1	1	2	2	1	12	9	7	6	4	4	3	3	2	3	5.0	5.3	4.9	5.3
Convergence criteria																			
EMU	−3	−3	−3	−3	−3	60	60	60	60	60	5	5	5	3	4	11.0	10.4	9.7	10.2
ECCU	−3	−3	−3	−3	−3	60	60	60	60	60	...	...	...	...	...	...	...	...	...
Number of countries meeting criteria																			
EMU	2	2	4	5	5	2	3	3	4	5	3	2	3	4	3	3	3	2	3
ECCU	2	2	4	5	5	2	3	3	4	5	...	...	...	...	...	...	...	...	...

Sources: IMF, World Economic Outlook database; national authorities; and IMF staff calculations.

Public debt levels remain high in the Pacific island region, and there is uncertainty about the long-term sustainability of the consolidation to date. IMF work on debt sustainability analysis for "poor performers" sets thresholds in net present value terms of 30 percent of GDP.[4] In the Pacific island region, all but Fiji and Samoa are classified as poor performers.

Additional fiscal convergence criteria used in other currency unions would be difficult for many countries in the region to meet. These include keeping the ratio of the wage bill to tax revenue below 35 percent and keeping financing of public investment from domestic revenue at above 20 percent of tax revenue.

Many currency unions include inflation and interest rate objectives. In the European Monetary Union (EMU), the inflation criterion is tied to the outcomes of the best-performing members, and in other currency unions the annual inflation target ranges from 3 to 10 percent. About half of the Pacific countries would meet the most stringent criteria and would also converge with Australia's inflation rate. The EMU also sets convergence criteria on interest rates, whereby the average nominal annual interest rate on 10-year benchmark government bonds should be no more than 2 percentage points above the average of the three best-performing member states. Only about half of the Pacific island countries would meet this convergence criterion, with almost 9 percentage points difference in lending rates between the highest (Solomon Islands) and lowest (Fiji).

Convergence of financial sector structure and stability is another precondition for a successful currency union or dollarization. This is a means to allow policy decisions to be synchronized and to minimize potential losses imposed by countries with weaker financial systems. The Pacific region's financial systems are relatively sound, in part because of the presence of foreign-owned banks. Financial supervision has been considerably strengthened in recent years, including through the efforts of the Association of Financial Supervisors of Pacific Countries and the Australian Prudential Regulatory Authority. At the same time, the level of financial development in the region is very low and formation of a currency union would promote the dismantling of barriers to intraregional capital flows and the establishment of regional capital markets.

At a more practical level, moving to a common currency or dollarization would require replacing all existing local currency liabilities of the central banks. This would entail having sufficient reserves or an agreed

---

[4]Poor performers are defined as those countries that fall into the bottom two quintiles of the World Bank's Country Policy and Institutional Assessment index measuring the quality of a country's macroeconomic policies.

currency swap with the anchor country to buy the existing local currency. All cash in circulation and in vaults would need to be exchanged, as would local currency government and commercial bank deposits with the monetary authorities. Currently, all the regional authorities, with the exception of Tonga, have sufficient reserves to cover the outstanding local currency liabilities of the monetary authority.

Concluding Remarks

This analysis suggests that the Pacific Island countries do not fully meet the criteria for a successful currency union or dollarization. Of particular concern are the costs that would be associated with the loss of the exchange rate as an instrument to adjust to terms of trade shocks and other external shocks, which are large in the region. At the same time, the potential benefits from improved credibility would be only modest. If the region were nonetheless to consider forming a currency union, it would make more sense to adopt the currency of an anchor country than to create a regional currency union with an independently floating currency, given the limited trade within the region. In this context, it would be more appropriate to adopt the Australian dollar than either the New Zealand or U.S. dollars.

If a decision is made to form a currency union, these countries will have to move a considerable distance to meet key convergence criteria. In particular, there are still large variances among them in public sector debt, interest rates, and exchange rates. Finally, creating a currency union or dollarizing would require in advance a strong political commitment to enhanced regional cooperation, and this will take time to achieve. Over the longer term, as trade in the region increases under PICTA, and as growth and inflation converge further, there may be growing benefit to the possibility of a currency union or dollarization.

II

COUNTRY NOTES

8

Fiji

Alain D'Hoore

Fiji is the second largest among the Pacific island countries, with a population estimated at about 840,000. Its total land area of 18,000 square kilometers is distributed among about 330 islands, a third of which are inhabited. Most Fijians live on the two main islands of Viti Levu and Vanua Levu. Fiji shares many of the challenges of other Pacific island countries, with its territorial fragmentation, remoteness from major markets, and a small, open economy with a high exposure to shocks such as commodity price fluctuations and natural disasters. The population, however, has a unique ethnic makeup, comprising ethnic Fijians (about 55 percent of the population); Indo-Fijians, the descendants of contract laborers brought by the British in the nineteenth century (down to about 40 percent from 50 percent in 1970); and other ethnic groups of various immigrant origins (about 5 percent of the population).

Latent political tensions between the two large ethnic groups have flared up in military coups on three occasions since the country's independence in 1970, after nearly a century as a British colony. Until 1987, a political party dominated by native Fijians won all general elections, and a party dominated by people of Indian descent constituted the opposition. Two military coups in short succession in 1987 interrupted the democratic process, following the election of a multiparty government perceived by the ethnic Fijian community to be Indo-Fijian dominated. The coups resulted in the return to power of native Fijians. Thirteen years later in 2000, following elections in 1999 that resulted in a new government led by an Indo-Fijian, another military coup was instigated. Parliamentary elections in 2001 restored an elected ethnic Fijian government, which was returned to power in elections in 2006.

Fiji is a lower-middle-income country, with per capita GDP estimated at $3,200. While only one-sixth of the land mass is suitable for agriculture, mainly along the coasts, this remains an important activity for a large part of the population, especially the cultivation of sugar cane on the main islands and copra on smaller ones. The main industries are sugar processing and garments. Services account for more than 60 percent of GDP, with recent growth in the high-end hotel and restaurant, transport, and communication sectors. The main foreign exchange earners remain sugar exports, mainly to the EU at preferential prices, and tourism, with the number of visitors now at 500,000 annually, the majority of which are from Australia and New Zealand. Recent years have seen growth in remittances from an emerging Indo-Fijian diaspora. Other exports include gold and garments, both on the decline, and timber and mineral water, mainly to the United States, Australia, and New Zealand. Fiji also serves as a regional hub in trade and transport among other Pacific islands.

Fiji scores well on a range of development indicators: life expectancy at birth is now close to 70 years; adult and female literacy rates are above 90 percent; close to 80 percent of the population has access to safe drinking water; and the immunization coverage is 95 percent. Yet there remain numerous challenges, as poverty remains high, especially in rural areas, and the rate of formal job creation is insufficient to absorb new entrants into the labor force. In addition, internal rural-to-urban migration, related mainly to structural issues in land and sugar policies, has put pressure on existing urban infrastructure and public services, relieved only in part by the outward migration of skilled Indo-Fijians.

Economic Experience since Independence

Fiji's per capita GDP almost doubled over the period 1970–2005, an annual average growth rate of 1.8 percent (Figure 8.1). The main spur to growth has been tourism, which is much bigger than in other Pacific island countries because of better airline connections with the main markets and substantially greater foreign direct investment. The overall growth experience is impressive considering Fiji's history of shocks, mainly cyclones but also droughts and floods, and the loss of skills to outmigration following the military coups.

Figure 8.1. Fiji: GDP per Capita
(1970=100)

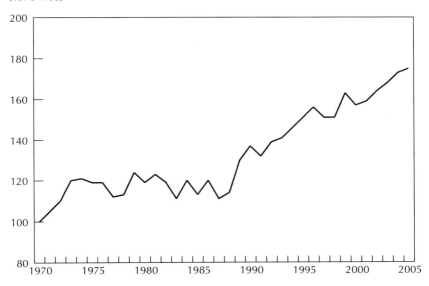

Source: IMF, World Economic Outlook database.

Outmigration, predominantly of skilled workers, has had a negative impact on human capital. Much, though not all, migration is related to political events. There is a clear trend of migration intensifying within the Indo-Fijian community, often among professionals, after independence, the coups in 1987, and the 2000 coup. The emigration of professionals has affected not only the business sector but also public administration, including the health system (almost 600 doctors are estimated to have left Fiji between 1984 and 1994) and public education (there has also been a significant outflow of teachers). Migration has brought an associated increase in remittances.

Fiji has been largely successful in taming inflation. There has been a gradual decline in inflation, from double-digit levels in the 1970s and early 1980s to the 0–5 percent range in the last 10 years (Figure 8.2). Fiji maintains an exchange rate peg against the currencies of its main trading partners. The rate was first readjusted against the peg in 1987, in the context of reserve losses associated with the coups (an 18 percent devaluation followed by a 15¼ percent devaluation). It was also adjusted in 1998, in the wake of the Asian crisis (a 20 percent devaluation). Also, starting in 1987, the central bank has chosen to maintain a fairly exten-

Figure 8.2. Fiji: Inflation
(In percent)

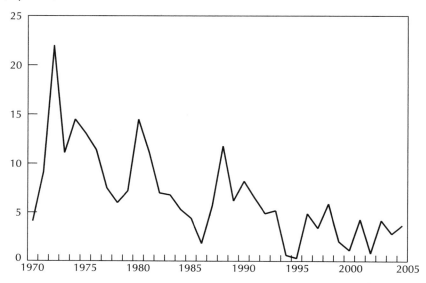

Source: IMF, World Economic Outlook database; and IMF staff estimates.

sive set of exchange controls, tightening them when pressures on foreign reserves have emerged.

During most of the post-independence period, successive governments have maintained an appropriate fiscal policy. The overall budget has generally been in deficit, though rarely exceeding 5 percent of GDP (Figure 8.3). On several occasions, this has required periods of tightening, which has normally been achieved by cuts in current expenditure, including the wage and salary bill. If the tightening has proved too unpopular, it has normally been reversed after a modest period.

As a result of the persistent deficits, there has been a gradual buildup of public debt, to over 50 percent of GDP at end-2005, even though public investment has not increased commensurately (Figure 8.4). Most debt is domestic, reflecting the growing capacity of the provident (pension) fund to take on more government-issued debt and Fiji's limited recourse to official development assistance since the political events of the late 1980s. Public debt has risen steadily, except during 1998, when a large, one-time repayment, funded from privatization proceeds, augmented a steep decline in the overall deficit to cut public debt by 18 percentage points of GDP.

Figure 8.3. Fiji: Overall Budget Deficit
(In percent of GDP)

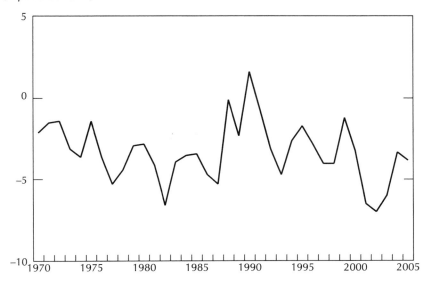

Source: IMF, World Economic Outlook database; and IMF staff estimates.

Developments in the 1970s and 1980s

During the 1970s, real GDP growth averaged 4–5 percent annually, with financial policies contributing to a stable macroeconomic environment. There was substantial foreign investment in tourism and a rapid expansion of sugar cultivation. Public investment, mainly in hydroelectric and water services, provided a boost in the latter part of the decade. Fiscal and credit policies were generally prudent. The overall balance of payments was in surplus in most years, with growth in sugar exports, tourist receipts, and concessional assistance more than matching the rapid growth of imports. In the mid-1970s, Fiji felt the impact of the worldwide recession and the first oil shock through decreased tourism and increased imports, although these were mitigated by a temporary surge in sugar prices.

During 1980–86, real GDP growth slowed markedly to 1–2 percent annually. The economy was buffeted by several shocks in this period, and large-scale public investment projects were completed. A sharp decline in the terms of trade caused a large fall in income, but fiscal and monetary policies were only gradually made more restrictive. A less restricted fiscal stance, with increases in real wages in the public sector, and accommodative

Figure 8.4. Fiji: Total Public Debt
(In percent of GDP)

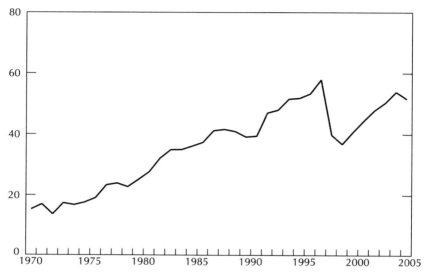

Sources: IMF, World Economic Outlook database; International Financial Statistics database; and IMF staff estimates.

monetary policy, which encouraged high credit growth, put pressure on the balance of payments. There was a tightening of policies in 1985–86, including cuts in public sector wages, but this contributed only modestly to restoring macroeconomic balance.

The 1987 military coups marked a watershed in Fiji's economic development. The first coup in 1987 led to a sharp drop in confidence, a fall in tourist arrivals, and a spike in capital outflows, while triggering a wave of migration by the Indo-Fijian community, whose net rate of population growth has been negative ever since. A second coup later in 1987 interrupted what had been a gradual return to normalcy. Economic policy was quickly shifted to containing the impact of the shock on the fiscal accounts—namely, by offsetting the loss in revenues and the increase in military spending—and on foreign reserves, which were also worsened by a drought-related drop in sugar exports. Discretionary spending was cut, including a wage cut and postponement of nonpriority investment projects.

The monetary authorities simultaneously shifted to a market-based instrument and tightened monetary conditions, partly by increasing commercial banks' refinancing rates at the central bank. Direct credit controls were also introduced as a precautionary measure, while interest rate controls were completely eliminated in 1987. The immediate objective of this move was to prevent deposit withdrawals in the wake of political disturbances and to contain rapid private sector credit growth. These measures proved unable to stem the reserve outflows, and so the authorities devalued the currency and, for the first time, introduced foreign exchange controls on various outflow transactions.

The interim civilian government that emerged after the coups undertook a profound shift in economic strategy to reignite growth. Its main elements included deregulation of the economy to align domestic prices more closely with world prices, restraining the growth of government spending, tax reform to improve supply incentives, and a civil service wage policy geared to maintaining external competitiveness. The government also pursued efforts to restore financial stability. In response to these measures, growth recovered, then gained further momentum in the following years.

Developments in the 1990s

Elections were held in 1992, and the new government continued to pursue the same broad economic strategy. Measures included liberalization of trade policies, with tariffs replacing licenses and quantitative restrictions; further tax reforms, with the lowering of some rates on business taxation and the introduction of a value-added tax (VAT); and attempts at deregulating the labor market. Fiji's average real GDP growth rate recovered to about 3 percent annually in the 1990s, but further increases were constrained by high migration and low private investment in the wake of the 1987 coups. In addition, shocks continued to hit the economy, including recessions in many of Fiji's trading partners in 1991 and a cyclone in 1993. The current account shifted into deficit, and gross international reserves declined, reaching a low at end-1993, before recovering in subsequent years.

In 1998, the authorities devalued the currency by 20 percent. They considered that the devaluation was needed to offset a real appreciation of nearly 10 percent during the previous years and to ward off future expectations of a devaluation in the wake of the Asian crisis. Underpinning the policy move was the realization that there was a need to offset continued pressure on the balance of payments arising from an increasingly loose fiscal stance (the overall deficit widened to more than 6 percent by 1997), which was designed to maintain growth despite the difficulties in the Asian region.

Developments since 2000

In 2000, Fiji's elected government was overthrown in a coup. In reaction, the British Commonwealth suspended Fiji's membership, and the international community applied economic sanctions, including postponement of development assistance projects. There were sharp declines in tourism earnings and tourism-related investment, overall investment, and textile exports, which contributed to a 3 percent decline in real GDP in 2000. Immediately following the coup, the central bank increased its lending rates sharply, imposed credit ceilings on bank lending, and tightened exchange controls to protect international reserves and relieve pressures on the Fiji dollar.

The Fijian economy recovered well. Real GDP growth averaged 3 percent annually between 2001 and 2004. Elections in 2001 led to the easing of official trade and aid sanctions and to Fiji's re-admission to the British Commonwealth. The main drivers of economic growth were a rebound in the tourism sector and an expansionary fiscal policy, with overall budget deficits of 6 percent of GDP during 2001–03 (much higher than the historical trend). At the same time, output growth stalled in the sugar sector, with the expiration of land leases, and there was a sharp fall in garment exports with the lifting of textile quotas in the U.S. market at the beginning of 2005.

Policy Challenges Ahead

Fiji faces a difficult medium-term outlook that could limit growth to about 2 percent annually as a result of the loss of garment export markets and the need to face a contraction of the sugar sector in 2007, when the European Commission has agreed to cut preferential prices under the sugar protocol. Even though sugar has lost much of its importance as a major source of export earnings in Fiji's balance of payments, the macroeconomic and social consequences of price cuts will still be significant. The focus of the government's sugar policy should include dealing with the politically difficult land lease issue, making domestic sugar pricing more sensitive to global markets, and providing assistance to rural households most affected by the income shock.

In addition, renewed political tensions could hinder the country's potential for sustained growth. Structural reforms are also needed. These include promotion of private sector activity through simplification of the investment approval process, dismantling of price controls, the elimination of distortionary import licenses, and a resolution of land issues.

Budgetary efforts should be geared toward restoring a low deficit. Most efforts need to come from the expenditure side, but there is scope for revenue gains, including by rationalizing the business environment with the elimination of numerous tax concessions for investment. Difficult measures will be necessary to reduce the weight of wages in total spending over the medium term, improve spending flexibility, achieve a better spending mix, and make room for needed public investment.

To achieve these fiscal goals and improve the provision of public services, there is a need to enhance the efficiency of public administration. The authorities have embarked on a program of administration reforms since 1999, with the adoption of a model framework with enhanced line agency accountability, strengthened incentives for performance, and supporting reforms in financial management systems. However, implementation needs to be strengthened despite capacity constraints.

9

Kiribati

Tarhan Feyzioğlu

The Republic of Kiribati consists of 33 islands straddling the equator. All the islands are coral atolls, with the exception of Banaba, which is of limestone origin and once had rich phosphate deposits, although these were exhausted in 1979, just at the time of independence. Whereas Kiribati's total land mass is very small, the exclusive economic zone (EEZ) that surrounds the islands is 3.5 million square kilometers, far larger than that of any other country in the region.

Kiribati gained independence from the United Kingdom in 1979, and its constitution provides for a government that combines parliamentary and presidential systems. The unicameral House of Assembly has 40 members elected for four years by universal adult suffrage, plus one ex officio member (the attorney general) and one member representing a community of Banabans who settled in Rabi, Fiji after the phosphate mine closed. The president is head of both the state and the government, is elected nationally, and selects his or her ministers from among the members of parliament.

Kiribati's population has increased rapidly, from 58,000 in 1980 to an estimated 90,000 in 2004. One-third of the population resides in South Tarawa, the capital and seat of government, and several of the outer islands are uninhabited. The population is young and the workforce is growing rapidly. This is especially true in the capital because of migration from the outer islands. Emigration is limited, except that around 2 percent of the workforce participates in an internationally recognized seamen certification program that provides temporary work opportunities abroad in international shipping.

Figure 9.1. Kiribati: GDP Growth
(In percent)

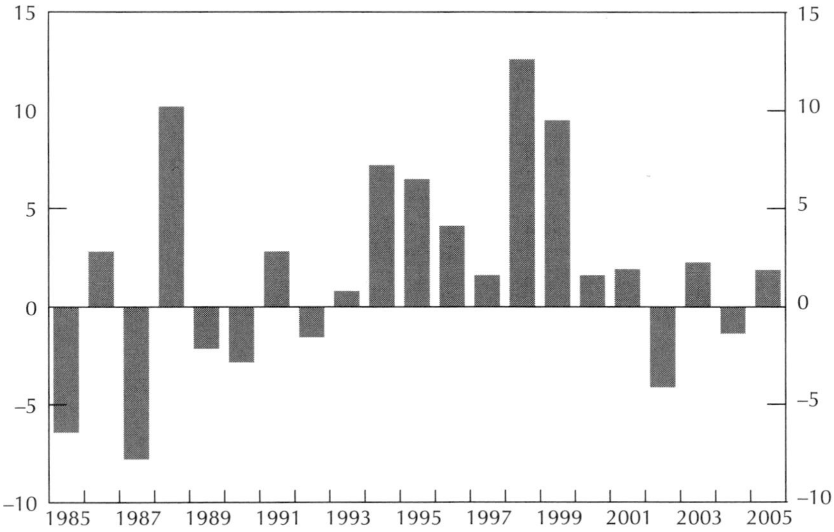

Source: Kiribati authorities.

The country is one of the smallest and least developed economies in the world. Its per capita GDP has remained stagnant since independence, and its total output is only about $70 million. Kiribati has very few natural endowments. The islands have shallow topsoil and low water absorption capacity, which allows the cultivation of very few crops. The main agricultural product is copra. As noted, the phosphate deposits on Banaba are exhausted; they had previously accounted for roughly 80 percent of export earnings and 50 percent of government revenue. There are vast marine resources, but these have brought only limited benefits, primarily from license fees paid by foreign fishing vessels.

Economic Profile since Independence

From independence until the mid-1990s, there was little growth, no manufacturing activity, and wide fluctuations in GDP, which reflected the economy's dependence on copra and on the fish catch (Figure 9.1). In some years, partly because of weather conditions, strong growth in one product compensated for a decline in the other. In other years, when the cycles

Figure 9.2. Kiribati: Copra Production
(In thousands metric tons)

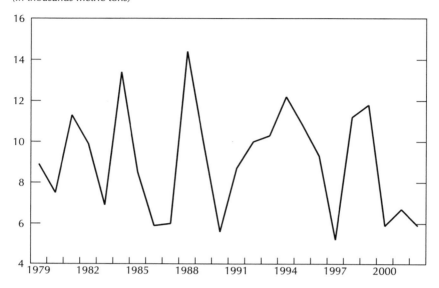

Source: Kiribati authorities.

were synchronized, there were large booms or busts. Overall, there was little progress in achieving sustainable growth during this period.

The government took a number of steps to boost copra production, with only limited success (Figure 9.2). Periodic subsidies to copra producers were financed by two funds, one that was replenished during good harvest periods and another supported by grants from the EU. In addition, the government distributed improved planting materials and provided extension services to spur replanting in an effort to lower the average age of the coconut trees and increase farms' productivity. However, the replanting targets were repeatedly scaled down because of growers' reluctance to forgo current income in order to invest in new trees. Shipping continues to be costly and cumbersome because of the lack of deepwater ports and infrequent service to foreign markets.

The domestic fish catch, the other mainstay of the economy, has also been highly volatile. There is a small fleet for deep-sea tuna fishing, and private households largely engage in subsistence fishing. The fluctuations in the fish catch reflect not only the weather conditions but also the condition of the fishing fleet. Poor maintenance leads to breakdowns of the fishing vessels. These problems have been compounded by the continual financial difficulties facing the state-owned fishing company, which have hampered the timely maintenance and repair of vessels, and by the limited access to export markets in the absence of storage facilities and regular commercial air transport links.

Tourism has been constrained by the country's remoteness, poor flight services, and the lack of knowledge about Kiribati in the major markets of Japan and the United States. There remains great potential for specialty tourism, such as birding, diving, and sport fishing. In fact, bird-watchers began to visit Christmas Island in the early 1990s, when reliable weekly service was established to and from Honolulu, three hours' flight away, but the air connections did not prove profitable for the national airline. As a signal to the private sector to take the lead in developing the tourist trade, the government offered for sale the main hotel on Christmas Island and later the hotel in South Tarawa, but neither has yet been privatized.

Until 1995, fiscal policy was consistently prudent, designed to promote the development of infrastructure without incurring deficits. Budgetary spending was restrained in order to reduce public services to a level sustainable in the post-phosphate era. Specifically, current expenditure was reduced from close to 70 percent of GDP at the time of independence to 50–55 percent in the mid-1980s, particularly through the compression of real wages of government employees, and was maintained there until the mid-1990s. Capital expenditure was primarily limited to projects financed by external assistance, particularly in the areas of transportation, fresh water, sewage, shipping, and telecommunications. As a result, there was either an overall surplus or a small deficit almost every year until the mid-1990s.

This prudent fiscal management, by successive governments, helped Kiribati persistently increase the value of its Revenue Equalization Reserve Fund (RERF), which was a stock of external assets built up in anticipation of the exhaustion of phosphate resources, primarily using royalties on phosphate exports (Box 9.1). Following the exhaustion of the phosphate deposits, government revenue declined by about half. On independence, the value of the RERF was equivalent to several years of imports of goods and services. It grew consistently because the authorities drew down only earned interest and dividends, while the principal increased in value as a result of buoyant international capital markets.

Kiribati's balance of payments was sound through the 1980s and early 1990s because of these prudent fiscal policies. Although exports represented only a small fraction of total imports, the current account remained in surplus reflecting the cautious domestic policies and the resultant increase in investment income. In addition, there were several important sources of

Box 9.1. Kiribati: The Revenue Equalization Reserve Fund

The Revenue Equalization Reserve Fund (RERF) was established in 1956 to hold royalties from phosphate mining in trust, anticipating the depletion of the deposits. The buildup of these savings occurred despite the lack of any explicit rule to safeguard the value of the RERF. Fiscal policy is not subject to any explicit rules, and there is no dedicated legislation governing the RERF. The 1979 Public Finance Act, Kiribati's budget law, set out general principles to guide government investments, but there is no requirement governing the size of drawdowns to finance current expenditure, and the government does not need parliamentary approval to increase drawdowns above budgeted levels. However, in 1996 parliament agreed in principle to hold the RERF's expected real per capita value constant for future generations. The use of the Australian dollar as domestic currency and the absence of a domestic debt market preclude other sources of domestic financing.

Prudent fiscal management by successive governments helped increase the value of the RERF until 1995. In the second half of the 1990s, the strong performance of the global equity market helped further boost its value. Between 1997 and 2000, average drawdowns were limited to 5.6 percent of GDP per annum, resulting in a 55 percent real increase in the value of the assets per citizen.

Starting in 2001, budget expenditure began to rise more quickly than revenues, and the growing deficit required a large drawdown. In 2001, expenditures rose sharply and budget financing from the RERF rose to 13½ percentage points of GDP despite near-record levels of revenues. During 2001–03, the correction in the stock markets caused the rate of return to turn sharply negative. In 2004, the drawdown to finance the deficit reached 24½ percent of GDP, although the increase in world stock prices still led to an overall increase in the size of the fund. Subsequently, because of persistent drawdowns and negative average rates of returns, the real per capita value of the fund has declined.

foreign exchange, namely, fishing royalties from foreign vessels that were licensed to fish in the EEZ, private transfers from workers abroad, and external aid. As a result, external reserves rose in most years and remained at comfortable levels.

Kiribati's use of the Australian dollar as its domestic currency has helped to underpin economic stability. The country did not establish a central monetary authority and imposed no exchange controls. Inflation, on average, has reflected price changes in major trade partners, in particular Australia. In 1984, the Bank of Kiribati commenced operations as the only bank, with government majority ownership, taking over the functions provided since 1970 by a branch of an Australian bank. The Bank

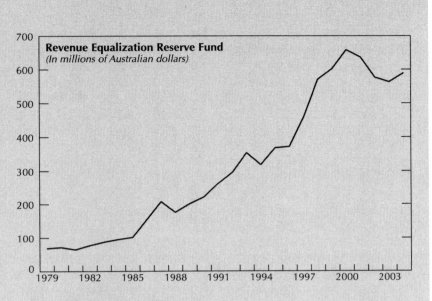

Revenue Equalization Reserve Fund
(In millions of Australian dollars)

Source: Kiribati authorities.

If current policies continue, the RERF could be depleted. Further drawdowns will be needed if growth continues to stagnate, population growth continues at current levels, the return on investments matches the long-term yield on Australian government bonds, and inflation converges to the Australian level of 2½ percent. Without corrective action, simulation exercises suggest that the RERF could be halved in 13 years and depleted in 24 years.

of Kiribati invested most of its assets abroad because of the negligible use of credit by the public sector and the management's perception that there was a shortage of viable lending opportunities in the domestic private sector. Interest rates on most types of deposits were generally comparable with those prevailing in Australia.

In 1995, in a major break with past conservatism, the government shifted to a more activist and unsustainable fiscal policy. Current expenditure increased substantially as large wage increases and the creation of two government ministries raised the wage bill, while subsidies and transfers also increased sharply (Figure 9.3). By 1996, the budget had moved to a deficit of 35 percent of GDP, requiring large drawdowns from the RERF.

Figure 9.3. Kiribati: Current Expenditures
(In percent of GDP)

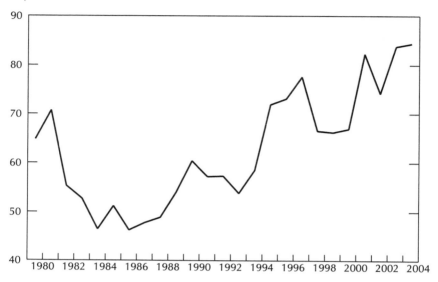

Source: Kiribati authorities.

Reflecting the expansionary government spending, GDP growth tem-porarily picked up and the current account went into deficit. Construction activity and government services increased, and the higher civil service wage bill increased household disposable income and consumption. Agriculture, domestic fishing, and manufacturing activities, on the other hand, remained stagnant or weakened. Imports of goods and services remained strong, even though there was a fall in exports and service receipts (in particular, fishing license fees), and the current account dete-riorated from a surplus of around 15 percent of GDP in the early 1990s to a deficit of 27 percent of GDP in 1996.

There was a temporary closing of the large budget and current account gaps in 1997–98 because of a large increase in revenue from licenses for tuna fishing in the EEZ. A strong El Niño weather pattern boosted the catch in Kiribati waters, and fishing license revenue jumped to almost 60 percent of GDP (Box 9.2). The budget balance improved to a surplus of 24 percent of GDP, and there was no need for drawdowns from the RERF. Even though current expenditure remained very high at more than 65 percent of GDP, the external current account surplus surged to

39 percent of GDP in 1998, in part because remittances from seamen grew rapidly.

Large budget and current account deficits subsequently reemerged, however, as public expenditure increased further and revenue from fishing licenses retreated to more usual levels. Current government expenditure rose consistently from 66 percent of GDP in 1998 to 84 percent of GDP in 2004, because personnel costs surged following increases in both public sector wages and the size of the workforce; higher subsidies to public enterprises, including large outlays for the lease of a commercial aircraft; and higher expenditure on locally purchased services. Development expenditure also increased sharply and exceeded the increase in external grants. The fiscal position deteriorated further to a record 41 percent of GDP in 2004 when expenditure cuts, mostly in development spending, proved insufficient to offset the continuing decline in revenue. Reflecting these developments, the current account deficit deteriorated to 16 percent of GDP.

The government began to draw heavily from the RERF as its fiscal situation deteriorated. In 2001, budget financing rose sharply to 13 percent of GDP. By 2004, drawdowns doubled to 25 percentage points of GDP. The persistent drawdowns and negative average rate of return over the 2001–04 period resulted in a marked decline in the real per capita value of the RERF. This was despite a 1996 decision by the parliament to keep constant for future generations the RERF's expected real per capita value. However, the 1979 Public Finance Act set only general principles to guide investment, and the government therefore did not need parliamentary approval to increase drawdowns above budgeted levels.

Economic growth came to a halt during 2000–04. Despite increases in government services and in construction related to development expenditure, growth was constrained by poor agricultural performance, especially a sharp decline in copra production after 1999, and by lack of improvements in the fishing fleet and support services. Various infrastructure problems also emerged periodically, notwithstanding increased spending in this area financed by external grants, especially for power generation, transportation, and telecommunications. Job creation in the formal sector remained limited. An increasing share of the labor force found employment in the subsistence, informal, or household sectors.

The lackluster economic performance after 1995 stems from a number of structural policy weaknesses. These include a large public sector that drew the country's scarcest resource—skilled labor—away from other productive activities and crowded out the private sector, an inefficient tax system, an unclear system of land titles, price controls, government subsidies,

Box 9.2. Kiribati: Fishing License Fees

Kiribati has a very large exclusive economic zone (EEZ), covering over 3 million square kilometers of tuna-rich waters. Given the country's very limited fishing capacity, revenue comes mainly from fishing license fees paid by foreigners, including from Korea and Taiwan Province of China. Fees are negotiated under bilateral agreements with all countries except the United States. In general, the license fees are around 5 percent of the value of the catch, but are sometimes negotiated together with grant aid and may thus be lower. The multilateral agreement with the United States covers the fishing waters of Kiribati and 15 other nations. Most of the fees are paid at the end of the year based on where the fish were actually caught.

Exogenous factors influence the amount of fishing license fees received in a year. Since 1990, there has been strong growth in revenues, but also substantial volatility. For example, revenues increased from $A 4 million in 1990 to a record of $A 47 million in 2001. However, the volumes caught depend on climatic conditions. In general, favorable El Niño weather patterns produce larger catches. International prices also determine the value of the catch and thus revenue levels, which also contributes to the volatility of fees.

To safeguard revenues and the environment over the long run, attention must be given to changes in fish stocks. In the near term, overfishing is not a major issue, because the bulk of the catch is skipjack tuna, which has not shown signs of declining stocks. However, the more highly priced yellowfin and bigeye tuna stocks have been declining, and this may eventually lead to reduced revenue. Regional cooperation is essential to safeguard the sustainability of stocks.

Over the medium term, there may be scope for Kiribati to develop its own capacity based around private commercial fishing businesses because the value of fish caught could generate substantial profits. Experiments with state-

limited competition in the financial sector, and complicated procedures for foreign direct investment. Other, non-policy-related factors also continued to constrain growth, such as Kiribati's remoteness from international markets and the wide dispersion of its population.

Future Policy Challenges

Absent a change in policies, growth will likely remain sluggish and the fiscal position unsustainable. With the population growing at close to 2 percent per year, in the absence of stronger growth, per capita GDP will

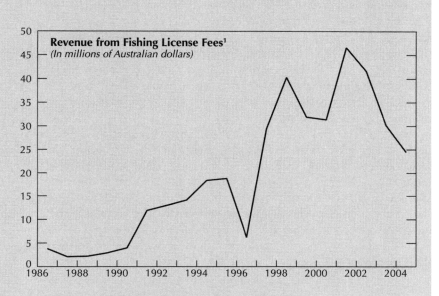

Revenue from Fishing License Fees[1]
(In millions of Australian dollars)

Source: Kiribati authorities.
[1]El Niño years: 1991–94; 1997–98; 2001–02.

run fishing enterprises, in Kiribati as in other Pacific island countries, have resulted in substantial losses. However, more than 1,000 Kiribati citizens work aboard foreign fishing boats and have substantial experience in the industry. The government could seek to attract investment in onshore processing, including by foreign enterprises with market access.

fall even further and unemployment will rise. Moreover, budget deficits are likely to increase, because a large share of total revenue is nontax revenue and grants and because expenditure pressures will rise with a growing population. Such deficits would require continued drawdowns from the RERF, putting the fund's value on a declining trend and eventually exhausting it.

Fiscal adjustment is needed to restore long-run macroeconomic stability. Budgetary efforts should be geared toward stabilizing the real per capita value of the RERF for future generations, which has been the stated policy since the fund's inception. The amount of fiscal consolidation required is sizable and will likely take several years of adjustment. In the near term, most of the adjustment must come from the expenditure side, because tax revenue is constrained by the limited growth in economic activity. The difficult measures that need to be taken include reducing the size of the wage bill, better targeting copra and seaweed subsidies, and strictly limiting development spending to the amount of donor grants. In parallel, it is necessary to lay the groundwork for a modern, efficient tax system. Establishing a medium-term fiscal framework would allow the government to track revenue trends over time and to identify periods of above-average revenues, which can be saved.

Structural reforms will be critical to generating growth. The government should give priority to reforms mentioned in the recent National Development Strategy, including streamlining public sector activities and increasing their efficiency, and creating an enabling environment for private sector growth and employment. In particular, commercial enterprises that are not monopolies should be privatized, where possible, to avoid crowding out private firms. Regulatory and financial oversight of noncommercial public enterprises should be enhanced with a view to increasing their efficiency.

10

Marshall Islands

HALI EDISON AND DAN NYBERG

The Republic of the Marshall Islands (RMI) consists of a group of atolls and islands in the central Pacific with a total land area of 20,000 square kilometers and 750,000 square miles of ocean. Two-thirds of the population of about 58,000 live in the two major urban centers, Majuro and Ebeye. Like other small Pacific island countries, the country is remote from major markets, and the economy is highly dependent on U.S. financing provided through the amended Compact of Free Association (covering 2004–23). Economic activity is dominated by the public sector, and a small private sector developed mainly to meet the demands of the government and its workers. Small contributions also come from agriculture, fisheries, and tourism. As a result of large external assistance, economic conditions are relatively favorable by regional standards, with a per capita GDP of around $2,500.

Politics and Government

In 1947, the Marshall Islands became part of the United Nations Trust Territory of the Pacific Islands, under the administration of the United States. Following increasing demands for autonomy, the country became a republic in 1979. The Compact of Free Association with the United States came into effect in 1986, under which RMI has full responsibility for its internal and foreign affairs, while the United States retains responsibility for defense and security. The United States also agreed to provide financial assistance totaling some $620 million over the period 1986–2001 and to create a $150 million Nuclear Trust Fund to compensate the inhabitants of the four atolls affected by U.S. nuclear tests in the 1940s and 1950s.

The government operates under a mixed parliamentary and presidential system, which includes a head of state, the president, and a bicameral parliament. The Council of Iroij (the upper house) is comprised of 12 tribal chiefs who advise the presidential cabinet and review legislation affecting customary law or any traditional practice, including land tenure. Legislative power resides in the Nitijela (the lower house), which consists of 33 senators elected by 24 electoral districts by universal suffrage of all citizens above 18 years of age. The president is elected to a four-year term and appoints cabinet ministers with the approval of the Nitijela. Although there are no restrictions on the formation of political parties, formal political parties do not exist. Instead, there are loosely formed interest groups that have no party headquarters, formal platforms, or party structures.

Human development indicators have lagged behind countries with similar income levels, despite high amounts of foreign aid and high health and education expenditures. Mortality rates for infants and children under age five are high compared to averages for middle-income countries and, according to the Human Development Index, RMI ranks in the bottom half among the Pacific island countries.

Structure of the Economy

Like most other Pacific islands, RMI faces a variety of geographical constraints, including limited land area, poor soil, territorial dispersion, and remoteness from major markets. Other obstacles include the acute shortage of skilled labor and a customary land tenure system, which severely limits the use of land as collateral in financial transactions and deters foreign investment. The outer islands operate on a semi-subsistence basis, while the urban centers of Majuro and Ebeye have a more developed cash economy, based mainly on government services and trade. The domestic production base is limited, consisting primarily of copra production, subsistence farming, fishing, and handicrafts.

The public sector plays a dominant role in the economy, backed by external assistance. Government current expenditure accounts for more than 70 percent of GDP, and about 50 percent of government revenue comes from external grants, mainly from the United States. Consequently, overall economic activity is highly correlated with government expenditure and external grant flows.

The public sector comprises the central government, local governments, trust funds, and nonfinancial public enterprises. The central government continues to be heavily dependent on foreign aid, while the main source of local government revenue is sales taxes. The government acts as trustee for a number of trust funds associated with the Compact, although the receipts and expenditures are largely outside the government budget. The largest of these is the Nuclear Trust Fund, set up to compensate inhabitants of the four atolls affected by U.S. nuclear testing, and the Kwajalein Atoll Trust Fund, which compensates landowners for the use of the atoll as a military base. Nonfinancial public enterprises are concentrated in utilities, transport, telecommunications, and copra production and are important sources of employment, but their financial results have been generally weak.

The private economy remains underdeveloped, primarily providing services to the government. The export sector is small, consisting almost entirely of coconut oil, fish, and reexports of diesel fuel to fishing boats. Nearly all raw materials and consumer and capital goods are imported. With exports amounting to about 20 percent of imports, the trade balance is chronically in deficit. Owing to official transfers, however, the current account balance has generally been in surplus or close to balanced (Figure 10.1).

There is no central bank, as the U.S. dollar is the domestic currency and the sole legal tender. The use of the U.S. dollar has imparted monetary stability, with inflation largely mirroring that of the United States. The real effective exchange rate has remained broadly stable, reflecting the low and stable inflation differential with the United States, RMI's largest trading partner. RMI is not competitive relative to other countries in the Pacific in terms of the costs of conducting business, especially for tourism, because of its geographical isolation and limited hotel facilities.

The banking sector is characterized by high intermediation costs and low levels of lending. Consumer loans account for the dominant share of loans and are primarily used for construction, travel, and education. Most consumer loans are serviced directly through payroll deductions. Longer-term lending is constrained by the land tenure system, which prevents banks from using land as collateral, as well as by the lack of viable projects. Given the limited opportunities to extend credit domestically, a substantial portion of the total assets of commercial banks is held outside the country.

Employment opportunities have not expanded at the rate of population growth. Continuously reliable data on unemployment are not available. According to the latest official survey, unemployment stood at around 30

Figure 10.1. Marshall Islands: Trade and Current Account Balances
(In percent of GDP)

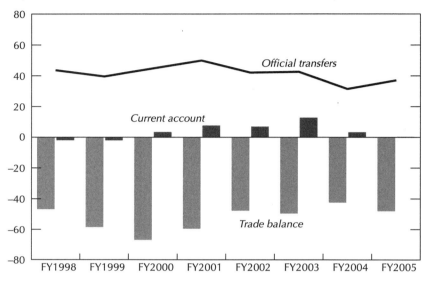

Source: Marshall Islands authorities.

percent in 1999, with youth unemployment considerably higher. While access to both primary and secondary education has improved recently, around 30 percent of children do not receive secondary education and dropout rates are high, contributing to the acute skills shortage. Emigration to the United States is relatively easy, and many Marshallese (around 15,000) have emigrated.

Economic Developments during Compact I, 1987–2003

The original Compact of Free Association with the United States (Compact I) aimed at fostering economic development over a 15-year period. The Compact provided block grants that were partially indexed to inflation and subject to step-downs in assistance after each five-year period. RMI also received earmarked grants and program assistance, mainly for health and education, with some conditionality and oversight attached to the grants. The limited scope for monetary and exchange rate policies underscored the key role of fiscal policy. Despite the large external aid, real GDP growth in RMI during the first Compact was the lowest

Figure 10.2. Marshall Islands: Real GDP
(Index 1987=100)

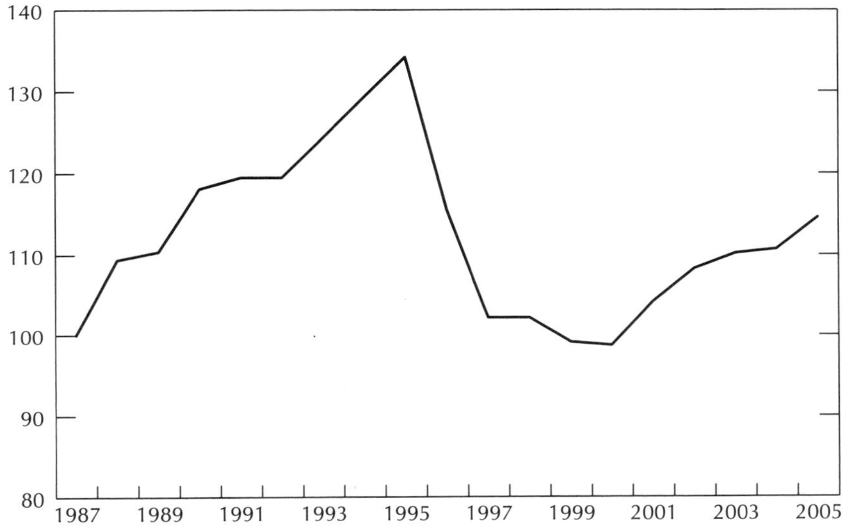

Sources: IMF, World Economic Outlook database; and IMF staff estimates and projections.

among all Pacific island countries except for Papua New Guinea. The two step-downs, after each five years, had substantial impact on real GDP.

Real GDP grew relatively quickly during 1987–91, averaging 4.5 percent annually, mainly reflecting Compact-related spending (Figure 10.2).[1] The public sector, already large as a legacy of the Trust Territory period, expanded further with the release of Compact funds. Capital spending to modernize the infrastructure picked up sharply. The private sector served mainly government demand and the growing ranks of public sector employees. Inflation pressures were generally contained.

In the first five years of the Compact, the government ran sizable budget surpluses, averaging 9 percent of GDP. With the first scheduled decline in grants, fiscal deficits began to appear in the early 1990s, averaging 10 percent of GDP during 1991–95. Although the reduction in U.S. aid was largely foreseen, government expenditures were not adjusted accordingly. The government borrowed sizable amounts abroad through medium-term notes, secured by future Compact flows, to finance deficits and fund public

---

[1]Except where noted, references are to fiscal years, which run from October 1 to September 30 (e.g., FY 2006 began on October 1, 2005).

Figure 10.3. Marshall Islands: External Debt
(In percent of GDP)

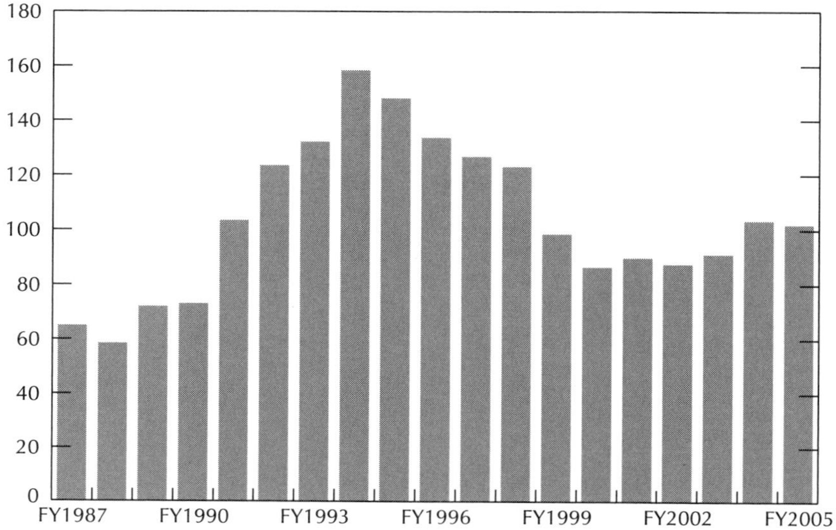

Source: Marshall Islands authorities.

investment. External public debt reached over 150 percent of GDP in 1995 (Figure 10.3). In addition, poor-performing public enterprises, including the national airline and the copra processing company, required subsidies that further drained government finances.

By the mid-1990s, the level of public expenditures and external debt had become unsustainable. Faced with the second scheduled decline in external grant assistance in 1996, the authorities implemented a public sector reform program. However, this consolidation, together with the impact of a drought, resulted in a large contraction, and real GDP declined by 5 percent on average during 1995–99.

After a five-year fiscal consolidation period, the economy rebounded, with real GDP growth averaging 3 percent annually in 2000–03. Adding to the rebound, during the 2002–03 negotiation of the amended Compact, the U.S. government provided so-called bump-up grants at the average level of the first Compact, a sizable increase over 2001. These funds helped to sustain the economic expansion and brought about an improvement in the overall fiscal position, even as some of the earlier progress in government consolidation was reversed.

Looking back, Compact I brought limited results in terms of real GDP growth, while fiscal and structural adjustment remained incomplete. A 2000 U.S. General Accounting Office report reviewed the effectiveness of Compact funds in promoting economic self-sufficiency and found that such expenditures had led to little improvement in economic development. In particular, real per capita income, adjusted for inflation, had fallen since the beginning of the Compact. The report also noted that funds were mainly spent to maintain high government wages and a high level of public employment that discouraged private sector growth.

In comparison with other Compact countries, RMI grew more slowly than Federated States of Micronesia and lagged well behind Palau. Tax revenue remained low due to long-standing weaknesses, and the wage bill was high. Public sector wages, set high to attract qualified personnel, were increasingly out of line with private sector pay and spurred migration from the outer atolls. Moreover, there were slippages in the administration of Compact funds, including shortcomings in accountability and oversight on the part of both the RMI and U.S. governments.

Economic Prospects during Compact II, 2004–23

The amended Compact came into effect in 2004 and will expire in 2023. U.S. funding will remain constant in nominal terms, with annual declines in grants fully offset each year by progressively higher contributions to a trust fund. The Compact grants target six specific sectors: education, health care, public infrastructure, the environment, public sector capacity building, and private sector development, with priority given to education and health. The Compact Trust Fund will be built up with installment contributions from the United States, RMI, and Taiwan Province of China. The main objective of the trust fund is to help achieve budgetary self-sufficiency in the post-Compact era, and no drawdowns or collateral borrowing are permitted until 2024.

Compact II also contains enhanced measures of accountability and monitoring (Box 10.1). A U.S.-RMI Joint Economic Management and Financial Accountability Committee was established to approve grant allocations and review performance outcomes and audits. Compact II allows for the possibility that the U.S. government could withhold funds in the case of noncompliance with grant terms and conditions. Adjusting to this enhanced accountability and monitoring is posing near-term challenges because capacity constraints have already led to delays in the disbursement of some Compact grants. Other provisions of the amended

Box 10.1. Marshall Islands: Comparison of Compacts I and II

The original Compact of Free Association (Compact I) came into effect in 1986. The three goals for RMI were to (i) secure self-government, (ii) ensure certain national security rights, and (iii) assist in efforts to promote economic self-sufficiency. The United States provided $640 million in grants during 1986–2001, with declining block grants every five years. These funds were provided to cover general government and capital expenditures. At least 40 percent of the total grants were to be devoted to capital projects, although this was a cumulative requirement that did not have to be satisfied in any particular year. Annual reports were required on economic performance and grant usage, and consultations were held to review the reports. Compact I also contained provisions allowing citizens of RMI to easily migrate and work in the United States. A provision specified that, if a new funding agreement was not in place by the time of expiration of the original Compact in 2001, aid would be given for an additional two years at the average level of the first 15 years ($42 million) (the so-called bump-up grants).

The amended Compact (Compact II) came into effect in 2004 and continues economic assistance during 2004–23. The total amount of $42.7 million per year (roughly 40 percent of GDP) includes grants, audit funds ($0.5 million), and trust fund contributions.

Grants target six specific sectors: education, health care, public infrastructure, the environment, public sector capacity building, and private sector development, with priority given to education and health. In addition to providing sector grants, the amended Compact provides for the establishment of a Compact Trust Fund that is intended to become a sustainable source of revenue to replace grant assistance beginning in 2024. RMI is required to provide $30 million to set up the trust fund, and the United States is to make an initial contribution of $7 million and then to further augment that by $0.5 million annually. Sector grants decline by that same $0.5 million per year in nominal terms.

New procedures were introduced to enhance financial accountability and economic management. A U.S.-RMI Joint Economic Management and Financial Accountability Committee was established to approve grant allocations and review performance outcomes and audits. Compact II allows the U.S. government to withhold funds in the case of noncompliance with grant terms and conditions.

Other provisions of the amended Compact include:

- Rental payments for U.S. military use of the Kwajalein Atoll through 2066, with the United States having the option to either terminate payments as early as 2030, with advance notice of seven years, or extend its use through 2086.
- An extension through 2023 of some education and disaster management services received by RMI under Compact I.
- A slight tightening of immigration provisions, with visitors to the United States from RMI now required to show a passport.

Compact include rental payments for U.S. military use of the Kwajalein atoll and an extension through 2023 of some education and disaster management services provided under the original Compact.

Real output growth remained modest at the beginning of the Compact II period. Economic activity was hampered by delays in implementing an upgraded public works program. However, civil service employment appears to have increased, primarily as a result of increased spending on education and health in line with Compact II. The government made large contributions to the Compact Trust Fund in 2003 and 2004, amounting to around 10 percent of GDP each year, in line with Compact II requirements.

The outstanding external debt remains high, although about 60 percent is on concessional terms and is owed primarily to the Asian Development Bank. The remaining 40 percent is mainly owed by two utility companies in telecommunications and energy. Against the background of declining Compact grants, servicing the external debt will absorb increasing levels of fiscal resources.

Policy Challenges Ahead

The major policy challenges are to achieve stable economic growth and financial independence. The 20-year Compact II agreement provides an opportunity to promote budgetary self-reliance and lessen RMI's dependence on foreign aid. At this point, the medium-term outlook remains uncertain and hinges on the authorities' commitment to structural and fiscal reform. In the absence of structural reform to promote fiscal consolidation and private sector activity, growth is likely to falter in the medium term, owing to declining Compact grants and increasing external debt repayments. However, if fiscal consolidation and structural reform are undertaken, RMI can grow sustainably and on a par with other Pacific island countries, even after the expiration of Compact II in 2023.

Fiscal Reforms

Budgetary surpluses are needed annually to ensure fiscal sustainability over the medium term. Achieving consolidation will require revenue-enhancing measures in combination with a substantial reduction and reorientation of current expenditure. Policies need to be implemented to reduce the payroll and to focus increases in development projects in the priority sectors identified in the Compact. Subsidies to public enterprises need to be curtailed, with a view to increasing economic efficiency. On the revenue side, measures should be taken to broaden the tax base, bolster tax administration, simplify the tax structure, and eliminate the cascading effects of sales taxes. A more comprehensive reform of the tax system could be considered in the medium term, perhaps through the introduction of a VAT or consumption tax.

An alternative scenario, without implementation of a medium-term fiscal adjustment, would lead to low economic growth and lack of budgetary self-sufficiency by the end of Compact II. In these circumstances, RMI would likely draw heavily from the trust fund after 2023, causing the fund to decline in real terms. By contrast, the adjustment scenario would be designed to ensure that only limited withdrawals are needed from the trust fund to maintain its real value after 2023 with economic self-sufficiency.

Structural Reforms

Structural reforms need to complement the fiscal reforms to encourage private sector development. The focus should be on clarifying property and land tenure rights, changing existing minimum-wage legislation to increase wage differentiation among skill levels, trimming extensive state involvement in business through privatization, and reducing constraints on foreign investment.

Development of the tourism sector continues to be hampered by RMI's distance from major markets, competition from lower-cost destinations, limited tourism infrastructure, and infrequent air service. The minimum wage is high by regional standards, which skews competition for jobs in the private sector and encourages migration from the outer atolls. The government has repeatedly launched public enterprises in areas such as fisheries and outer island shipping that have lost money and competed directly with private firms. Bank lending continues to be limited by the difficulties of using land as collateral and of foreclosing. In order for the banking system to play a full role in the development of the economy, longer-term bank lending needs to be facilitated by improvements in the newly established land registry.

11

Micronesia

CHARLES KRAMER

The Federated States of Micronesia (FSM) comprises about 600 islands, stretching 1,800 miles across the central Pacific. The total landmass of about 700,000 square kilometers is spread over a sea area of 1 million square miles, including its exclusive economic zone. With the remote location, small population of 110,000, and narrow resource base, Micronesia has much in common with other Pacific island countries. Economic and social conditions are relatively favorable by regional standards, with per capita GDP of around $2,000, primarily because of very high external grants under the two successive Compacts of Free Association with the United States (Box 11.1). At the same time, there is a need for major adjustment efforts because external assistance will be reduced in coming years.

Political Background

Micronesia was formed from part of the United Nations Trust Territory of the Pacific countries, which was administered by the United States after the end of World War II. The four states of Kosrae, Pohnpei, Chuuk, and Yap signed a constitution in 1979 and attained independence in 1986. These states had much in common: each was isolated, had poor transportation links and a narrow resource base, and engaged in little trade within or beyond the region. Growth was impeded by a lack of infrastructure, particularly in air, shipping, water, sewer, and power services, as well as by the

Box 11.1. Micronesia: Compacts of Free Association with the United States

The economic assistance provisions of the original Compact covered 1987–2001. It provided annual cash grants of $97.9 million during 1987–91, $91.1 million during 1992–96, and $79.2 million during 1997–2001. The funds were to cover general government and capital expenditures, with the latter to comprise a minimum of 40 percent of grants. During the 2002–03 interim, while the Compact was being renegotiated, grants were provided at the average level of the initial Compact period (so-called bump-up funds), which represents a sizable increase from immediately preceding years.

The renewed Compact II covers 2004–23 and features declining grant assistance, creation of a trust fund, and enhanced accountability and monitoring:

- Total funding: Total funding of $92.7 million per year comprises primarily grants and trust fund contributions. Grants are $76.2 million during 2004–06, after which they decline by $0.8 million per year in nominal terms, to $62.6 million in 2023. Grants and trust fund contributions are indexed at the lesser of two-thirds the increase in the U.S. GDP deflator or 5 percent.
- Compact Trust Fund: Trust fund contributions are set to rise from $16 million in 2004 to $29.6 million in 2023. In addition, Micronesia made a $30 million contribution in 2004, as required under Compact II. The trust fund cannot be used to finance spending or as collateral for borrowing before 2024. The fund is administered by a five-member committee (three U.S. and two FSM appointees) and can invest in U.S. stocks and bonds and other instruments as approved by the committee.
- Accountability and monitoring: A U.S.-Micronesia Joint Economic Management Committee approves grant allocations and reviews performance outcomes and audits. The committee is composed of three U.S. and two FSM members.
- Sectoral allocations: Funds are to be allocated to six priority sectors—health, infrastructure, education, capacity building, environment, and private sector development. There are no explicit formulas for allocation by sector, but the committee has resolved that infrastructure spending should rise toward at least 30 percent of annual Compact grants by 2006.
- Other provisions: Disaster assistance from the U.S. Federal Emergency Management Agency is to be phased out over time and replaced by assistance administered through the U.S. Department of State. Funding under certain U.S. educational programs is to be replaced by the Supplemental Education Grant (about $12 million in 2005). Immigration provisions are tightened; for instance, visitors now must show a passport, but access to emigration and U.S. jobs remains relatively straightforward.

poor educational and health systems. Formal markets, including financial markets, were underdeveloped; land ownership revolved around customary arrangements; and foreign investment was minimal. Accordingly, subsistence fishing and farming played an important role.

In other aspects, the four states were highly diverse. They had distinct cultures with individual languages and tribal structures. They were geographically varied, with some comprising low-lying atolls and others featuring high volcanic mountains. Moreover, each state had its own executive, judicial, and legislative branches, as did the new national government. Under this system, although the national government has statutory authority for policy coordination, in practice the states exercise considerable autonomy in economic affairs. The constitution gives the national government the power to levy taxes on income and imports, while reserving for the states the authority to levy sales and other taxes.

Economic Developments: Compact I, 1987–2003

Compact I came into effect in 1987.[1] It covered a 15-year period, with a possible two-year extension, and aimed to foster economic development and financial independence. As a main mechanism for achieving this end, the Compact provided block grants that were only partially indexed to inflation and were subject to cuts (step-downs) each five-year period. Micronesia also received earmarked grants and program assistance, mainly for health, education, and welfare. In principle, some conditionality and oversight were attached to the grants. At least 40 percent were to be devoted to capital projects, although this was a cumulative requirement that did not have to be satisfied in any particular year. Annual reports were required on economic performance and grant usage, and consultations with the U.S. government were mandated to review the reports. The Compact also allowed citizens of Micronesia to easily migrate to and work in the United States.

The country registered satisfactory real GDP growth of 3.6 percent annually during 1987–95, reflecting two related developments. First, the public sector, already large as a legacy of the Trust Territory period, swelled in tandem with the sizable grants provided under the Compact. Public sector real output rose by a cumulative 27 percent over this period, while employment increased by 15 percent in the public sector (including

---

[1]Except where noted, references are to fiscal years, which run from October 1 to September 30 (e.g., FY 2006 began on October 1, 2005).

national, state, and municipal governments plus public enterprises). As part of this trend, capital spending to modernize the infrastructure picked up sharply. Second, resources were drawn out of the informal sector into the market economy. This development was related closely to the growth of the public sector, because the formal private sector served mainly to support the burgeoning government and the swelling ranks of public sector employees. Although the growth of the public sector had beneficial spillovers to the private sector, it brought difficulties as well. Public sector wages were high, in order to attract qualified personnel, and were out of line with private sector pay, making it difficult for the private sector to compete for skilled workers. In addition, the government launched public enterprises in such areas as pepper, fisheries, and coconut processing, and these lost money and competed directly with private firms. In some instances, notably the case of the Development Bank, the existence of public enterprises was rationalized by impediments to private sector activity, such as restrictions on land ownership. However, the failure to tackle these impediments directly served to further dampen private sector activity, which grew only very modestly.

The sizable investment in infrastructure did make services more accessible and reliable. However, the heavy expenditure on government administration and business ventures failed to foster economic development. Moreover, there were slippages in the administration of Compact funds, including misuse of funds and shortcomings in accountability and oversight on the part of both the FSM and U.S. governments.

On the positive side, macroeconomic stability was broadly maintained. In the early years of the Compact, the government ran sizable budget surpluses, partly because capacity limitations acted to restrain spending. Inflation pressures were contained, and use of the U.S. dollar as the domestic currency and the sole legal tender imparted much-needed monetary stability, with no adverse impact on competitiveness. However, the limited scope for monetary and exchange rate policies underscored the crucial role of fiscal policy in meeting the burden of economic adjustment.

Fiscal deficits began to appear in the early 1990s, averaging about 3 percent of GDP during 1992–93. The government borrowed considerable amounts abroad through medium-term notes secured by future Compact flows, in order to finance the deficits and fund public investment, and external public debt reached 72 percent of GDP in 1993. In addition, exports remained weak, at less than a quarter of imports, and comprised mainly fish and agricultural products. With only modest tourism receipts, the external current account, excluding grants, was in deficit. Nevertheless, Micronesia smoothly weathered the first step-down in Compact funds that

Figure 11.1. Micronesia: GDP Growth and Inflation
(In percent)

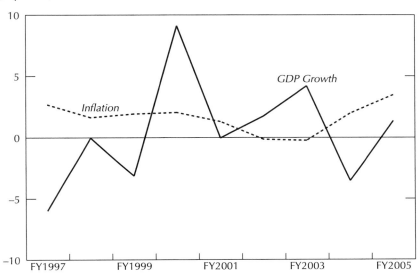

Sources: Micronesia authorities and IMF staff estimates.

occurred in 1992 despite the weaker budgetary and external positions, mainly because of limited spending capacity and its external borrowing.

With absorptive capacity improving and external borrowing already large, adjusting to the second step-down in Compact funding in 1997 proved more difficult. Real GDP declined by 3.5 percent annually during 1996–99, offsetting the gains in the earlier five-year period (Figure 11.1). Faced with reduced external assistance, the national government decided to scale back its workforce. It launched a public sector reform program, under which two years' salary could be paid to employees to induce early retirement. The reform program also involved cutbacks in working hours, which had been rising substantially. As a consequence of these steps, the wage bill was reduced by 29 percent by 1999. Public enterprise reforms were also initiated, and outlays for subsidies were reduced by about a third. However, these measures were only partly successful and the fiscal situation remained difficult, with the budget moving from near balance in 1995–97 to deficits of over 7 percent of GDP in 1998–99. Moreover, private sector activity remained sluggish, even though the external current account had moved to surplus by 1999 (Figure 11.2).

Figure 11.2. Micronesia: Current Account and Fiscal Balances
(In percent of GDP)

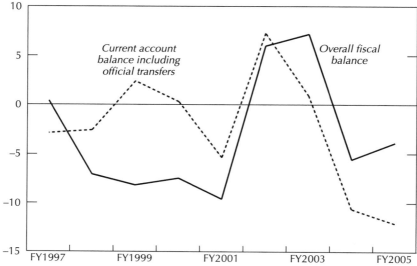

Sources: Micronesia authorities and IMF staff estimates.

Growth rates varied considerably among the four states, as well as between urban areas and outer islands within each state. Fiscal discipline also was uneven across the states, and slower growth tended to increase the fragility of their respective financial positions, particularly when tax measures and expenditure cuts were postponed. This was most notable in Chuuk, where fiscal mismanagement triggered a crisis in the mid-1990s. Specifically, persistently high expenditures exhausted the state's cash reserves, leading to arrears that in 1996 peaked at 30 percent of state GDP. Subsequently, the Chuuk government embarked on a stabilization program with conditional financial support from the national government and also launched an early retirement program to bring the wage bill under control. By 2000, most or all of recorded arrears had been cleared. Pohnpei also faced a liquidity crisis in the late 1990s because of inadequate controls on spending.

Given the dominant economic role of the public sector and the role of the Compact in financing it, the step-downs and concomitant adjustments have had a major adverse impact on economic activity. This has prompted emigration, and, accordingly, population growth slowed from 2 percent to about ¼ percent per year. By 1999, an estimated 12,000 Micronesian citizens, or more than 10 percent of the population, had emigrated, mainly to Guam and Hawaii, while an unknown but probably large number had emigrated to the continental United States.

With the country's economic performance deteriorating and viable investment opportunities scant, one commercial bank decided to cease operations in Micronesia, prompting a prolonged decline in outstanding credit. The bank offered to sell its loan portfolio to the remaining two commercial banks, but they expressed little interest, mainly because of a perceived excessive level of risk.

By the turn of the century, the effects of fiscal adjustment were waning and the economy was rebounding, with real GDP growth averaging 3.7 percent annually in 2000–03. During the 2002–03 renegotiation of the Compact, the U.S. government provided so-called bump-up funds, with grants set at their average level since 1987, which was significantly more than the 2001 level. These extra funds helped to sustain the economic expansion during the next two years and brought about an improvement in the overall fiscal position, even as earlier progress in government retrenchment was partially eroded. However, private sector activity continued to be sluggish, and the structure of the economy remained little changed from the beginning of the Compact period.

During the life of Compact I, real GDP growth averaged only 1.9 percent annually, and fiscal and structural adjustment remained incomplete. Micronesia enjoyed higher growth than the Marshall Islands, but both lagged well behind Palau, the third Compact country, especially in creating private sector employment (Box 11.2). Tax revenue remained low due to long-standing weaknesses, and the wage bill was high. Poorly performing public enterprises put a continual drag on public finances. The autonomy of the states and the absence of collective objectives compromised the formulation of fiscal and development objectives at the national level.

Yet these years also provided a hopeful message: effective policies can pay dividends in terms of growth and stability. The evidence came from Yap state, which had a record of both fiscal propriety and a relatively fertile environment for private enterprise. Yap achieved the strongest growth in the nation, with output rising by almost 50 percent cumulatively over 1987–2001, twice the average rate in the other three states. This suggested that, while the barriers to macroeconomic stability and economic development in the country might be sizable, they are not insurmountable.

Box 11.2. Micronesia: Comparison with Other Compact Countries

Micronesia, Marshall Islands, and Palau (all formerly part of the Trust Territory of the Pacific Islands) currently have Compacts of Free Association with the United States. The three countries have similar characteristics, with heavy reliance on official grants and dollarization. Nonetheless, cross-country comparisons highlight notable differences among them.

Compared with Marshall Islands, Micronesia has experienced higher GDP growth and enjoys higher GDP per capita at present. However, both countries have lagged behind Palau in terms of economic development, and a large part of their population is still in the subsistence sector. Furthermore, growth in

Nominal GDP per Capita[1,2]
(In U.S. dollars)

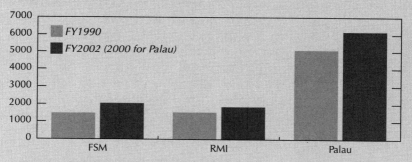

Sources: Micronesia authorities and IMF staff estimates.
[1]Although reliable GDP deflators for long periods are not available, inflation in Micronesia does not seem to be higher than that in other countries for these years.
[2]Data for Palau are for calendar year.

Private Sector Employment[1]
(In percent of population)

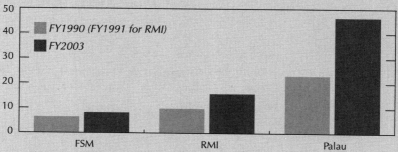

Sources: Micronesia authorities and IMF staff estimates.
[1]Data for Palau are for calendar year.

paid private sector employment has been modest. The differences in economic performances may be partly attributed to geography: Palau is closest to large Asian countries and receives the most international visitors. All three countries have enjoyed price stability during recent years, thanks to use of the U.S. dollar as the domestic currency.

Regarding fiscal performance, all three countries are characterized by low domestic revenue, high dependence on grants, and large current expenditures. As a share of GDP, Micronesia has the lowest domestic revenue, the highest grants, and the largest wage expenditures. That said, like Palau, Micronesia's government debt is at comfortably low levels, thanks to the large grants.

Fiscal Indicators (FY2003)
(In percent of GDP)

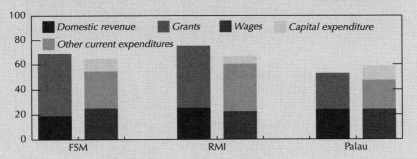

Sources: Micronesia authorities and IMF staff estimates.

External Debt
(In percent of GDP)

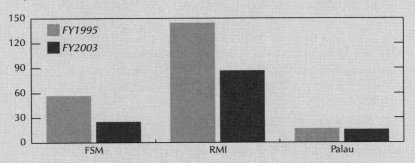

Sources: Micronesia authorities and IMF staff estimates.

Figure 11.3. Micronesia: U.S. Compact Grants
(In percent of GDP)

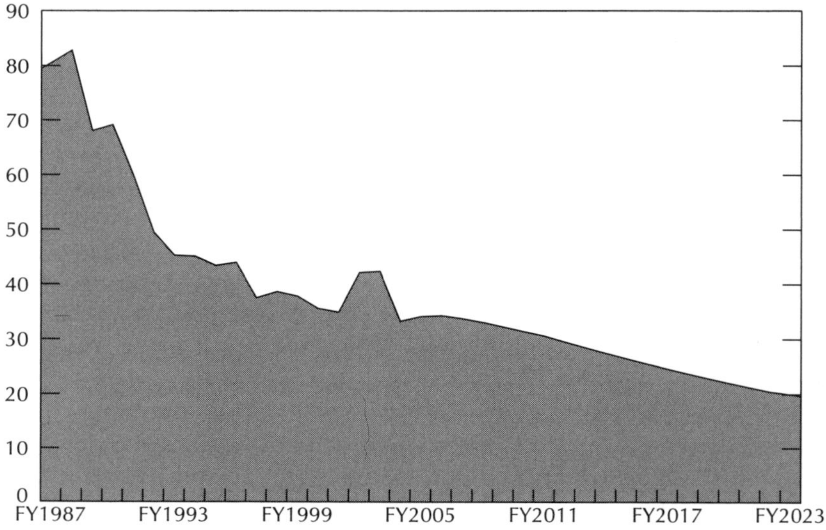

Sources: FSM authorities and IMF staff estimates.

Economic Prospects during Compact II, 2004–23

The amended Compact (Compact II) came into effect in 2004. Despite the periodic step-downs since 1987, grants remain sizable, amounting to one-third of GDP, or about $700 per capita. The grants will steadily decline until the Compact expires in 2023 (Figure 11.3). During this period, a trust fund will be built up with payments from Micronesia and the United States, and initial contributions have already been made by both parties. Throughout the period, total U.S. funding will be partly adjusted for U.S. inflation, with programmed declines in grants to be fully offset each year by progressively higher contributions to the Compact Trust Fund. The main purpose of the trust fund is to secure economic self-sufficiency in the post-Compact era, and no drawings or collateral borrowing is permitted until 2024.

There are two major features that differ markedly from Compact I. First, the amended Compact incorporates enhanced accountability, monitoring, and conditionality. A U.S.–Micronesia Joint Economic Management Committee has been established to review allocations and review performance outcomes and audits. Grant disbursement can be held up if requirements are not satisfied. In addition, resources are to be directed to six priority sectors: health, infrastructure, education, capacity building, environment, and private sector development. There are no explicit formulas for allocations by sector, but the committee has resolved that infrastructure spending should rise toward at least 30 percent of grants by 2006. Second, Compact II incorporates steady annual declines in grants (rather than discrete step-downs), with only partial indexation for inflation.

Making the adjustment to these two changes will be a major challenge, as will the ultimate goal of attaining stable economic growth and financial independence. In the near term, the challenge will be to adapt to the tighter conditionality. In 2004, a third of programmed grants, equivalent to 11 percent of GDP, could not be absorbed due to capacity constraints in meeting Compact requirements, although these funds were subsequently released, and a 2005 U.S. Government Accountability Office report found that there had been improvements in both accountability and monitoring. The larger challenge, and the main one facing Micronesia over the medium term, is achieving fiscal and economic sustainability in the face of a continuous decline in external assistance. Moreover, under existing arrangements, the trust fund may suffice only to replace expiring grants for a few years after the Compact expires.

To help promote longer-term sustainability, Micronesia will need to undertake sustained fiscal consolidation, as well as structural reforms to foster a more vibrant private sector. Early action toward these ends is vital to forestall major and disruptive adjustments later in the Compact period.

To ensure fiscal sustainability over the medium term, the government must realize budgetary surpluses annually. There are two major issues that must be addressed to achieve this degree of consolidation. First, tax revenues are low by regional standards at only about 11 percent of GDP, compared with over 15 percent in Marshall Islands and over 20 percent in Palau and the larger Pacific islands. There are persistent weaknesses in administration and compliance that need to be corrected. Beyond this, the system must be modernized and streamlined, including by removal of distortions created by cascading taxes through which goods are taxed at multiple stages (e.g., as imports, during production, and at final sale). One option for reform is introduction of a VAT similar to that adopted by a number of other Pacific island countries in recent years, and as recommended by the Presidential Task Force on Tax Reform. Implementation of a VAT would require the cooperation of the states, which have constitutional jurisdiction over consumption taxes.

On the expenditure side, despite continued wage and hiring freezes, the wage bill remains high compared with other Pacific island countries at about 25 percent of GDP. This is several percentage points above the levels in Marshall Islands and Palau, and far above the level in the larger Pacific island countries, including Fiji, Papua New Guinea, Samoa, and Solomon Islands. A lower wage bill is essential to meet Compact requirements for enhancing spending in key sectors, such as health, education, and infrastructure, as well as to support long-run growth. Public enterprises should be reformed to reduce their continuing burden on the budget. This sector remains significant in size, accounting for 5 percent of employment, roughly the same as all the main export-oriented sectors combined. Reducing the size of this sector would be consistent with the authorities' strategy to facilitate private sector development.

Fiscal reforms need to be complemented by structural reforms to encourage private sector development and employment. Issues that should be addressed include the high cost of doing business; poor infrastructure, with periodic power outages; obstacles to foreign ownership of land and to the use of land as collateral for loans; and an opaque and lengthy application process for foreign investment. The commercial banking system is sound, and the two private banks benefit from U.S. Federal Deposit Insurance Corporation (FDIC) oversight provided under the Compact. However, the banks invest primarily abroad, in view of the domestic risks associated with shortcomings in the legal framework and uncertain economic prospects. Their strong liquidity provides scope for greater lending, which would be stimulated by structural reforms. The present trade regime is relatively unrestrictive, and the commitment of the authorities to further liberalization under the regional trade arrangements is indicative of their intention to enhance private sector competitiveness.

12

Palau

Wafa Fahmi Abdelati

The Republic of Palau is an archipelago of more than 560 islands. It has a total land area of 460 square kilometers stretching along 700 kilometers of sea from northeast to southwest. The center of government and economic activity is the northern volcanic island of Koror, which is connected by bridge to Babeldaob, a densely vegetated island that accounts for 78 percent of total land area but remains largely undeveloped. The capital is to move from Koror to Babeldaob. South of Koror and scattered over a large lagoon are the 300-odd raised coral limestone Rock Islands, mostly uninhabited, and world-renowned for marine-based tourism. The southernmost islands of Peleliu and Angaur were the site of fierce battles during the Second World War. Palau was administered by the United States after the war and until 1990 as part of the United Nations Trust Territory of the Pacific Islands. Palau adopted its own constitution in 1981 after choosing not to join the Federated States of Micronesia in 1978. A Compact of Free Association with the United States was approved in 1986 but ratified only in 1993, following several referenda on whether the United States should be permitted to transport nuclear weapons through Palau's territory. Under the Compact, the United States controls Palau's security and defense for 50 years and has exclusive access to waterways and certain land, in exchange for economic aid, security, and right of entry for Palauans to the United States for residence or work (Box 12.1).

The government is based broadly on the U.S. model. The legislative branch of government is made of a bicameral parliament consisting of nine senators elected at large and 16 congressmen representing each of

Box 12.1. Palau: The Compact of Free Association

The Compact of Free Association is a 50-year political and economic treaty between the Republic of Palau and the United States. It provides for Palau to conduct its own domestic and foreign affairs while the United States retains control of defense and security matters as well as strategic access to specified land areas. The United States is to provide payments over the first 15 years of the Compact. The terms of the Compact and its related agreements are subject to review by both parties at specified intervals during its 50-year life, including to discuss its termination or extension. The Compact was agreed to in principle in 1986, and it took effect in 1994, when Palau became a sovereign nation.

Compact payments are a combination of rent and aid, amounting to nearly $600 million in total direct payments. About 80 percent of the cash amounts have been disbursed in the first 11 years. Compact funds comprise the following:

- The $70 million set aside for a trust fund to provide a stream of income until 2044 and beyond. Assuming a 12.5 percent rate of return, the trust fund was expected to provide sustainable withdrawals of $15 million from 2010, adjusted for inflation.
- Front-loaded grants in the first year of the Compact for current and capital improvements that are lowered in the second year and fifth year.
- In-kind grants amounting to $149 million for the construction of the Compact Road on Babeldaob Island.
- Services and programs of U.S. government agencies, such as the Federal Deposit Insurance Corporation, the Small Business Administration,

the states. There are no political parties. Tribal chiefs—including two high chiefs representing the northern and southern states—and high-ranking women play a traditional albeit diminishing role in land allocations and pose a challenge to policymaking. The president, elected for a four-year term on a separate ticket from the vice president, can introduce and veto legislation, while the parliament can overrule such vetoes. Policymaking is centered around the president's advisory body, which comprises the chief of staff, minister of finance (or his financial advisor), and a senior counsel.

The Human Development Index Score for Palau is the highest among the Pacific island countries. Per capita gross national income is estimated at $6,870, and the government spends around 11 percent of GDP on health and education. Nearly 93 percent of households have access to the Economic Development Association, the Rural Electrification Administration, the Job Corps; postal, weather, and aviation services; and services relating to tourism and marine resource development of the Department of Commerce.

The main objective of Compact grants is to establish an infrastructure base that will enable Palau to become self-sustaining by the end of the 15-year period (2009). Among the conditions of approval was adoption of an economic development plan that outlined particular goals and methods to achieve these goals. Among these goals was downsizing of the public sector, preserving the environment, and establishing a regulatory climate supportive of private sector activity. The government of Palau is required to report annually "on the implementation of the plans and on its use of the funds." The annual reports are subject to financial audits. In addition to Compact payments, Palau is eligible for other U.S. assistance, based on direct proposals to grantor agencies, which have amounted to an additional 6 percent of GDP annually in recent years. Palauans have the right to enter the United States and establish residence as nonimmigrants and accept employment, including in the U.S. military.

Palau's economic performance during 1994–2005 exceeded that of the other two Compact countries, Marshall Islands and Micronesia. Judicious management of foreign aid to build a capital base and public sector retrenchment helped establish a foundation for private sector growth. Solid progress was made in fiscal consolidation, even if much greater efforts are still needed. Private sector jobs nearly doubled and economic growth exceeded that of RMI and FSM despite the series of external shocks.

piped water, 98 percent have electric power, and 91 percent have telephones. High levels of sanitation, free pubic health services for citizens, and recent campaigns have supported health promotion and disease prevention, but changing demographics and lifestyles have increased the incidence of noncommunicable diseases, including cardiovascular illness, hypertension, obesity, and cancer. The dependency ratio has been falling due to high rates of emigration to the United States, a growing number of foreign workers without their families, and a declining fertility rate. The economy is heavily dependent on foreign aid, foreign labor, and tourism receipts, and is thus vulnerable to external shocks.

Palau is endowed with a uniquely diverse but fragile natural environment. The marine environment is home to endangered turtles, some 1,400 inshore fish species, and more than 800 coral species. The terrestrial environment includes 1,258 plant species (104 endemic) and 141 bird species. Economic development poses a number of threats, including sand and coral dredging, overfishing and illegal fishing practices, mangrove clearing, waste disposal, and overuse of popular sites by divers and other visitors.

Structure of the Economy

Palau faces a number of constraints common to small islands: a narrow production base, remote location, small size (population of 20,000), and limited resource base. The outer islands operate on a semi-subsistence basis, but most of the population—located in Koror and the adjoining three islands—caters to tourism and public sector services. Palau's fishing and tourism industries are vulnerable to hurricanes and fish migration patterns.

The public sector consists of the central government, 16 state governments, and a few nonfinancial public enterprises. The central government's domestic revenue comes from trade taxes (6 percent of GDP), salary and wage taxes (5 percent of GDP), a gross receipts tax (6 percent of GDP), other taxes (3 percent of GDP), and nontax revenue (6 percent of GDP). The main source of local government revenue is fishing fees, site fees from tourists, and block grant transfers from the central government. The nonfinancial public enterprises are concentrated in utilities and telecommunications and do not receive state subsidies. Health, education, water, and waste disposal are almost exclusively provided as public services. Government current expenditures amounted to 45 percent of GDP in 2005, and civil service wages remain high, at 22 percent of GDP.

Private sector activity is centered around tourism and government contracts, including construction. In spite of abundant marine life and fertile soil, agriculture and fishing account for less than 4 percent of GDP. Like other small island states, Palau is heavily reliant on foreign imports and has few local commodities to replace such goods or to export. Fish account for nearly all exports (9 percent of GDP). The lack of export capacity raises shipping costs and results in consistently large trade deficits. In 2004, visitor receipts reached an estimated 70 percent of GDP.

The U.S. dollar is used as the domestic currency and sole legal tender. There is no central monetary authority. Use of the dollar has brought stability, and most foreign assistance and trade flows are with the United States. The banking sector is large compared to the size of the economy. Palau currently has eight commercial banks, a development bank, and several credit unions, insurance companies, and remittance agencies. About 80 percent of deposits are held by branches of FDIC-insured U.S. banks, who invest about half these assets in the United States. Domestic lending is limited to small, salary-secured consumer loans. There is a large spread between deposit and lending rates, partly due to the high operating costs and low profitability of the two local banks, as well as country risk and the difficulty of using land as collateral for securing loans.

Uncertainty over property rights has been a major constraint on economic development. Most land was held on a customary basis prior to 1971. At that time, a titling process was initiated, including surveys of lots and efforts to determine ownership through the Land Courts (even once titles are granted, there are individual-to-clan disputes). By early 2005, nearly 60 percent of the 17,000 lots in the central land register had been surveyed and their ownership established. However, only Palauans can own land and only Palauan-owned banks can take land as collateral for loans. Foreigners can obtain leases of up to 50 years and foreign-owned banks can accept leases as security for loans. The constitution prohibits taxation of land.

Expatriates constitute over one-half the labor force. Over half of resident Palauans work in the public sector, and the remainder are employed in higher-paying private sector positions, including as professionals, managers, and technical and sales staff. Only about 14 percent of Palauans are employed in lower-paying service sector jobs, which are filled mainly by Asian expatriates. Taking advantage of easy entry, nearly one-third of Palauan citizens reside in the United States.

Economic Developments since Independence

Real GDP grew rapidly in the first three years under the Compact, averaging 8½ percent and buoyed by annual grants of nearly 100 percent of GDP. Public sector spending was the main driver of economic growth. Economic growth stagnated for the next seven years, due to the adverse effects of the Asian crisis in 1997–98, the September 11 events in 2001, and SARS in 2003. In 2003, real GDP stood below the 1996 level.[1] Growth picked up again in 2004, and inflation has remained low. GDP growth is estimated at around 5 percent annually during 2004–05, driven by a steady increase in visitor arrivals with the start of new airline routes and hotels

---

[1]Except where noted, references are to fiscal years, which run from October 1 to September 30 (e.g., FY 2006 began on October 1, 2005).

Figure 12.1. Palau: Trade and Current Account Balances
(In percent of GDP)[1]

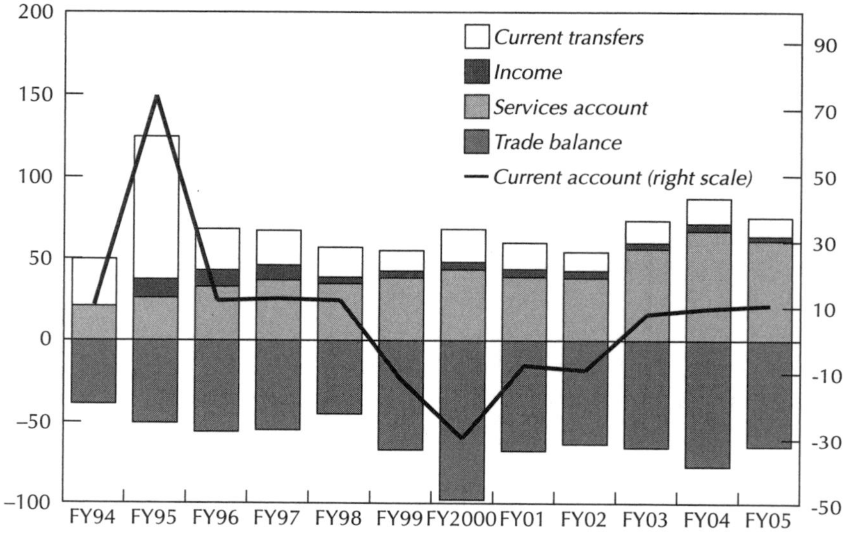

Source: Palau authorities.

and ongoing public infrastructure projects. The public sector's relative importance in the economy has declined since 1994, although it remains the major employer for Palauans. The growing expatriate community has helped develop the service sector, and growth in tourism and construction has allowed an increasing number of Palauan-owned businesses to undertake government contracts and start tourism service businesses that had previously been operated by expatriate firms.

Rising tourist receipts also have helped improve Palau's external position. The current account balance turned back into surplus in 2003 as the number of tourists more than recovered following the Asian crisis to reach new record highs (Figure 12.1). In addition, fish exports increased with the return of migratory species. The negative trade balance is now more than offset by service receipts.

Fiscal performance has improved since 2000. Domestic revenue increased from 22 to 27 percent of GDP, while the ratio of current spending to GDP declined from 60 percent to 45 percent as the result of a hiring freeze and cuts in nonwage spending. In the last four years, the current budget declined by 8½ percent of GDP owing to a cap on the rate of increase of nonwage current expenditure. After two years of negative returns, because of the decline in U.S. equity markets in 2000 and 2001, the Compact Trust Fund posted an average return of 9 percent in the following three years. However, the average return for the period 1994–2005 was 7½ percent, well below the 12½ percent return assumed at the time of the Compact agreement. Public debt stands at 13 percent of GDP, the lowest among the Pacific islands, as external borrowing has been prudently avoided. Palau's experience contrasts with that of the other two Compact countries, which did not adjust expenditures in anticipation of declining Compact grants and instead resorted to sizable government borrowing.

The banking sector came under scrutiny in 2001, when Palau was placed on the list of noncooperative countries by the Financial Action Task Force. It was removed soon after it introduced an anti–money laundering policy in 2001 by means of the Financial Institutions Act, Money Laundering and Proceeds of Crime Act, and Mutual Assistance in Criminal Matters Act. It also established a Financial Institutions Commission in 2002 and a Financial Intelligence Unit in 2003. A bank relicensing scheme reduced the number of commercial banks from 38 in the late 1990s to 8 in 2003. In spite of these improvements, implementation and oversight of the financial system remain weak due to understaffing, inadequate training, and insufficient budgetary resources. Moreover, the Palau Development Bank and some 15 remittance companies remain outside the scope of prudential regulation.

The cost of doing business in Palau is internationally competitive, but the regulatory environment prevents foreign investment in certain sectors. Since 1994, the foreign investment law has reserved the following activities exclusively for citizens: land transportation; wholesale and retail trade; tour guides, fishing guides, and diving guides; all forms of water transportation; travel and tour agencies; and commercial fishing for species that are not highly migratory. Activities that can be undertaken by foreigners only in partnership with Palauan citizens include handicraft and gift shops (under very limited circumstances), bar services not in a hotel or restaurant, manufacturing, equipment rentals for land and water, and any other business as may be determined by the Foreign Investment Board. In spite of these constraints, total foreign investment rose to about 13 percent of GDP in 2004. This reflects large investments in a new airline and a luxury hotel. There has been an ongoing debate in parliament and within the business community on the trade-offs among reducing restrictions for foreign investors, ensuring transparency, and protecting the interests of influential Palauan citizens. Formal employment has grown at an estimated 4½ percent annually since 1994, and the public sector's relative importance as an employer has declined substantially over the

Figure 12.2. Palau: Real GDP
(1993=100)

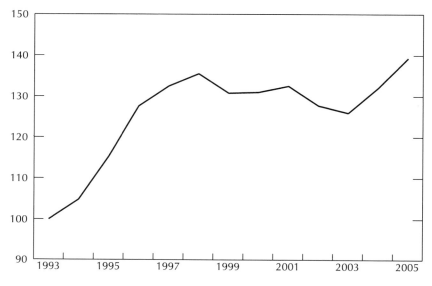

Sources: IMF, World Economic Outlook database; Palau authorities; and IMF staff estimates.

last decade. Employment has been growing at about 9 percent annually for foreign workers and 1½ percent annually for Palauans. Foreign workers are required to return home upon termination of their employment. Remittance outflows are substantial, estimated to be as high as 20 percent of GDP. Palau's performance exceeded that of the other two Compact countries in several ways. Judicious management of foreign aid to build a capital base and public sector retrenchment helped establish a better foundation for private sector growth. Solid progress was made in fiscal consolidation, although further efforts are still needed. The economy grew faster than that of Marshall Islands and Micronesia, in the face of a similar set of external shocks (Figure 12.2).

Economic Outlook and Policy Challenges Ahead

The key challenges facing Palau are to continue building an economic foundation for sustainable growth and to achieve financial self-sufficiency. Current spending must further decline to achieve fiscal sustainability. The remaining impediments to dynamic private sector activity should be addressed, and the banking sector should be strengthened to enhance financial intermediation. The economy faces substantial downside risks from the possible sharp reduction in U.S. grants and other program assistance. Palau expects its Compact to be renewed when it expires in 2009 in order to facilitate its transition to financial independence, but no decision has yet been reached with the United States. An extension would permit a more gradual fiscal consolidation and cushion the impact on growth, but prudence dictates continuing on the recent path of fiscal adjustment regardless of the likelihood of a Compact renewal.

Fiscal Sustainability

A substantial adjustment is needed to ensure fiscal sustainability over the long term. Increasing domestic revenues would require a comprehensive reform of the tax system to simplify and broaden the tax base through the introduction of a VAT or consumption tax and with respect to corporate and personal income taxes. On the expenditure side, contracting out of public services would help reduce the wage bill and spending on goods and services. If the Compact is renewed, the adjustment effort could be phased in more slowly while preserving the trust fund, although the resulting value of the fund would depend on the level of future Compact grants, and this will not be known anytime soon. In the meantime, continuing the consolidation efforts would improve the economy's ability to weather shocks and would demonstrate that Palau is serious about achieving financial independence.

Investment Climate

Continued efforts are needed to sustain the growth of tourism and foreign investment. This would be facilitated by removing restrictions on sectors open to foreigners, the availability of land for collateral, annual expatriate labor permits, and legal requirements to hire Palauan labor. Despite the current restrictions, however, the costs of starting a business are lower in Palau than in most other countries in the region (Figure 12.3), and the World Bank's "Doing Business" survey reports that operating costs for existing business ventures are low. A large supply of Asian labor has helped keep private sector wages from rising in the face of rising labor demand.

Palau hopes to add supply capacity in the high-end tourism market, building on recent success. This strategy is believed to be the best way to prevent the type of environmental degradation that can result from large

Figure 12.3. The Costs of Starting a Business in the Pacific Islands
(In percent of gross national income per capita)

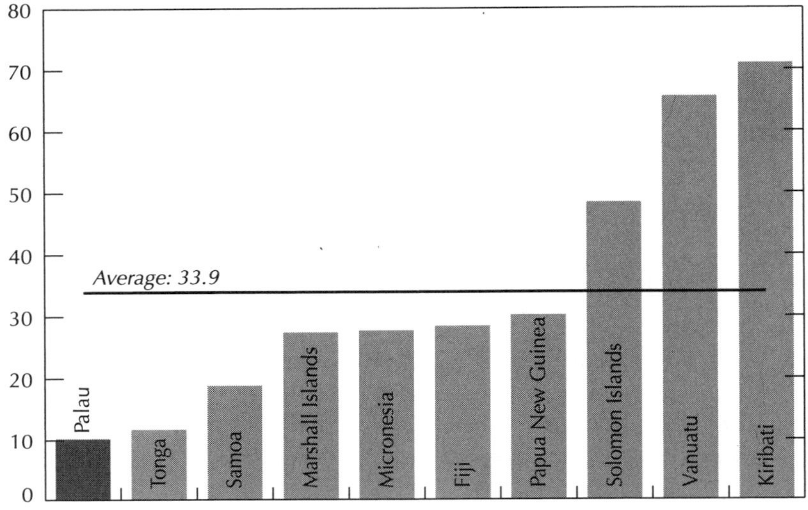

Source: World Bank, *Cost of Doing Business*, 2005.

increases in low-end tourism capacity. The tourism infrastructure compares well with other tourist-dependent economies in terms of accommodation capacity and profitability, as reflected in high tourist expenditures per capita.

Banking Soundness

Bank lending continues to be limited by the difficulty of both using land as collateral and foreclosing. In order for the banking system to play a larger role in the development of the economy, longer-term lending would be facilitated by expeditious titling of the remaining 40 percent of individual lots and of the state lands that can be leased. Introducing and implementing banking regulations would ensure that potential banking problems are detected and corrected at an early stage. Strengthening bank supervision would help local banks better compete with the foreign branches that are subject to U.S. oversight.

13

Papua New Guinea

PHILIPPE MARCINIAK

Papua New Guinea (PNG) is the largest (463,000 square kilometers) and most populated (5.5 million) of the Pacific island countries. The country's land area is scattered among some 600 islands, predominantly mountainous and covered with one of the largest tropical rain forests in the world. Despite a high population growth rate by regional standards (2.7 percent annually), population density remains among the lowest in the region. About 80–85 percent of the population live in rural areas, mostly on communally owned land and with considerable dependence on subsistence farming. The social structure is the most fragmented in the region, with some 700 different language groups, and this has strained political stability and social cohesion. Although the country has abundant natural resources, social and poverty indicators are the lowest in the region.

Papua New Guinea became independent in 1975. The government is based on the system of the United Kingdom. The 109-member parliament is elected for a five-year term, and the prime minister, who is selected by members, nominates the cabinet. Six general elections have been held since independence, and none of the prime ministers has so far completed a full five-year term, although the present government is expected to do so in 2007. The country's multiple political parties are based on loose and temporary alliances, and coalition governments have been the norm. Provincial governments, now numbering 19, were created shortly after independence.

Economic and social performance since independence has fallen short of potential, with per capita income in 2004 hardly above its 1975 level

Figure 13.1. Papua New Guinea: Nominal GDP per Capita
(1990=100)

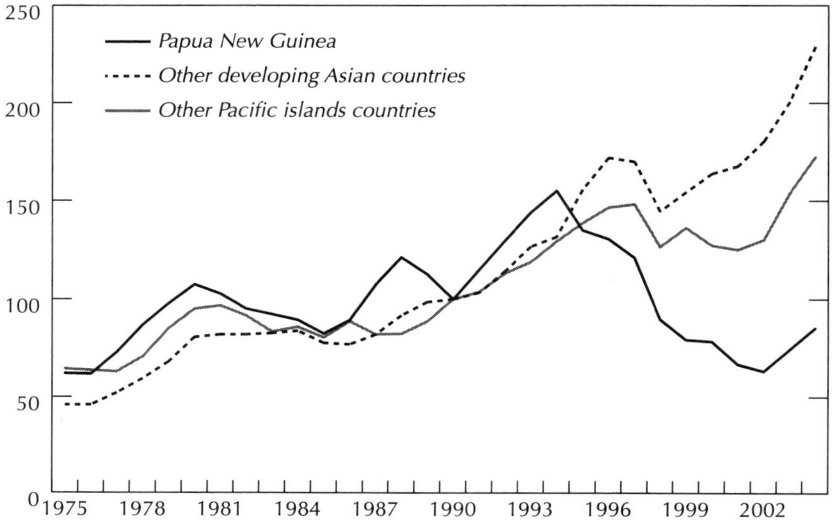

Sources: IMF, World Economic Outlook database; and IMF staff calculations.

(Figure 13.1).[1] In the years immediately after independence, large mineral discoveries were made, but growth remained modest (Box 13.1). During most of the 1980s, growth accelerated as these discoveries were developed. However, since the late 1980s, Papua New Guinea has faced a number of severe crises, including the closure of the Bougainville copper mine in 1989, a severe El Niño–related drought, the Asian financial crisis in 1997–98, two severe cyclones, and a major volcanic eruption. Since 2002, macroeconomic stability has been restored, the external position has strengthened, and growth prospects have improved.

---

[1]Ebrima Faal, "Growth and Productivity in Papua New Guinea," IMF Working Paper 06/113 (Washington: International Monetary Fund), examines Papua New Guinea's historical economic growth patterns through a simple growth accounting framework. The analysis shows that downward swings in growth are mostly accounted for by a significant slowdown in capital input and lower total factor productivity.

Economic Developments since Independence

Papua New Guinea's economic performance since independence has primarily mirrored mineral output cycles. Until the late 1980s, growth was stimulated by the impulse of the copper mines. In the 1990s, despite the mining and petroleum boom, fiscal deficits aggravated the impact of adverse shocks. Macroeconomic adjustments were supported by two IMF Stand-By Arrangements during 1990–92 and another in 1995, and these temporarily contained the deterioration in fiscal and external balances. Efforts to stabilize the economy and foster private-sector-led growth were renewed in 2000–01, supported by a fourth Stand-By Arrangement, but economic recovery failed to pick up. Further efforts to achieve sustainable growth were launched by the new government after the 2002 elections, and good progress was made in stabilizing the economy through fiscal consolidation in concert with supportive monetary policy and aided by a favorable external environment.

Economic Structure

Agriculture has remained the predominant contributor to income and employment, but its growth has been slow. Agriculture, including fisheries and forestry, now generates about 40 percent of GDP. The main export crops include coffee, cocoa, copra, and palm oil. The sector is dominated by small-holders who grow both subsistence and cash crops. Output performance has been constrained by a deficient feeder road infrastructure, inadequate technical and managerial skills, traditional land tenure, and law-and-order problems, which have inhibited marketing. The mineral sector (including petroleum) is a large contributor to national income and has been the main driver of economic growth since independence, presently accounting for about 20 percent of GDP. Its growth has been variable over the last three decades, reflecting the pace of new discoveries and wide fluctuations in international commodity prices. The initial impulse to development was provided by the Bougainville copper mine, which began operations in 1972. The mine, which initially generated nearly a third of the country's national income, was closed in 1989, in response to violent disputes with landowners. In the mid-1980s, mineral production was bolstered by the Ok Tedi copper mine. The 1990s witnessed a boom in the mineral and petroleum sectors, with production from the Kutubu and Gobe oil fields and several gold mines coming online. The Napa Napa oil refinery began production in 2004.

The manufacturing sector has failed to develop since independence. The sector, which accounts for about 6 percent of GDP, consists primar-

Box 13.1. Papua New Guinea: Mineral and Petroleum Sector Developments and Prospects

The mineral and petroleum sectors have been the main pillars of the country's development (accounting for 21 percent of GDP, 75 percent of exports, and 20 percent of tax revenue), despite high output volatility. The sector's contribution to employment has been limited, however. High exploration costs stemming from poor infrastructure, an unfavorable tax regime, government ownership constraints, protracted negotiations with landowners, law-and-order problems, and environmental concerns have restrained exploration and investment in the last decade. Prospects have improved since 2003, in response to strong world prices, mineral tax reform, and a renewed outlook for major gas and nickel projects, which all contributed to an upturn in exploration. The government has the option of taking a 30 percent equity in new mineral projects and 22.5 percent in petroleum and gas projects.

Gold and silver output (30 percent of exports) has been declining in recent years, reflecting lower output from two major mines (Porgera and Lihir). Gold is also mined by small operators and comes as a by-product of the Ok Tedi copper mine. Gold output is projected to drop further during the next decade, as production from new mines (Hidden Valley and Tolukuma) is not expected to fully offset the decline from existing mines. Silver is mined along with gold and copper ore; its output is projected to decline significantly from 2013, in line with Ok Tedi's dwindling output.

Copper output (17 percent of exports) is derived mainly from the Ok Tedi mine, which has been operating since 1984 and is expected to cease operations in 2012. The Australian majority owner gave its equity to the government in

ily of small firms producing for the domestic market. Development is constrained by the low-skilled labor force, by complicated regulations that inhibit private sector activity, and by high utility and transportation costs. The services sector includes sizable resources for public administration.

Progress during the 1970s and 1980s

External shocks in the early post-independence years were successfully cushioned by appropriate macroeconomic policies. Independence took place during the worldwide downturn that followed the first oil crisis. This resulted in a marked decline in demand for copper, the main source of growth and export earnings at that time. Inflationary pressures rose

2002 to settle litigation stemming from environmental issues. The Bougainville copper mine, which provided the country's main financial resources during 1972–89, was closed in response to civil strife initiated by landowners. The ensuing secessionist conflict ended in 2001, with the Bougainville province becoming autonomous in mid-2005. Prospects for its rehabilitation are bleak in view of the high financing requirement.

The Ramu Nickel project was finalized in 2005 under a joint venture with a Chinese company. Projected nickel and cobalt output are expected to significantly boost mineral prospects starting in 2010.

Petroleum output (25 percent of exports) from the Kutubu, Gobe, and Moran oil fields has declined steadily in recent years, and current reserves are expected to be exhausted by 2012.

Natural gas reserves are significant but have remained largely untapped. They are, however, expected to bolster development prospects upon completion of the long-delayed Queensland Gas Project, tentatively scheduled for 2009. Meanwhile, the critical mass of potential customers to make the project viable was reached in mid-2005. The project's front-end engineering and design phase is scheduled for completion in 2006. The project calls for the construction of a 2,655 km gas pipeline to Australia at a $3 billion total cost, of which $2 billion will be in Papua New Guinea. Average annual gas sales over the 30-year life of the project are valued at $800 million, providing large annual government revenue. The magnitude of government equity participation in the project and downstream projects and associated financing package are still under discussion.

in response to higher import prices. In addition, full wage indexation, inherited from Australia, contributed to labor market rigidities and hampered exchange rate management. Capital flight, the departure of many high-income and skilled foreigners, and land tenure problems adversely constrained recovery efforts. As a result, during the second half of the 1970s real GDP rose by only 1–2 percent annually.

Papua New Guinea recovered rapidly from the global recession triggered in the early 1980s by higher oil prices. Real GDP initially fell as agricultural production declined, mainly in response to lower export prices, and the rate of inflation rose sharply, mainly due to higher import prices. Recovery picked up from 1983, with real GDP growing at about 4 percent annually for the rest of the decade, largely in response to increasing mineral output.

Figure 13.2. Papua New Guinea: Fiscal and External Current Account Balances
(In percent of GDP)

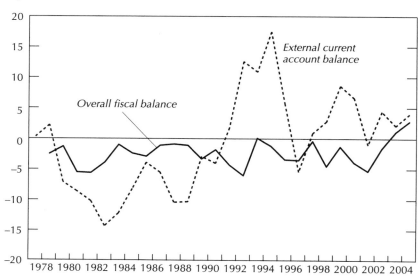

Sources: National authorities; IMF, World Economic Outlook database; and IMF staff calculations.

Terms of trade deterioration of 30 percent during 1980–82 caused large external current account deficits (Figure 13.2). In response, the government borrowed from external commercial sources, more than doubling external debt as a share of GDP. International reserves declined over the same period. The external current account position then strengthened and the trade account moved back into surplus, in line with the export recovery and the fall in mining sector imports. Financing the current account still required substantial private and official external borrowing. As a result, outstanding external debt rose to over 90 percent of GDP, and the debt service ratio reached 30 percent in 1985. With more restrictive demand management policies, this debt was reduced considerably during 1986–88 in relation to GDP.

Economic Problems during the 1990s

The closure of the Bougainville mine necessitated a macroeconomic adjustment effort during 1990–92, which facilitated stabilization of the external situation, with IMF financial support. The adoption of expansionary policies by a new government then caused the macroeconomic situation to deteriorate. In response, in 1995 the government adopted another adjustment program supported by a Stand-By Arrangement. Average real GDP grew by less than 1 percent annually in the second part of the 1990s, reflecting a lack of new mineral exploration activities, deterioration of the physical infrastructure in rural areas, the 1997 drought and consequent temporary closure of the largest copper mine, the contraction in foreign demand in the wake of the Asian crisis, and widespread governance and law-and-order problems. As confidence eroded, private capital outflows intensified, and the kina depreciated markedly despite central bank intervention. Inflation soared to the 12–20 percent range in 1998.

Budgetary deficits were sizable during the decade. The initial recovery was accompanied by an expansionary fiscal stance fueled by defense spending on Bougainville, tax reductions, subsidies on agricultural support schemes, and persistent expenditure overruns. Wider budget deficits were financed largely through central bank borrowing. Macroeconomic stability was restored in 1995–96, as outlays on goods and services and transfers to the statutory authorities were cut. However, spending growth resumed sharply ahead of the 1997 elections. Government debt rose to 60 percent of GDP in 1999, from 45 percent in 1990.

Several balance of payments crises emerged during the 1990s. Balance of payments performance in the early 1990s continued to be severely affected by the closure of the Bougainville copper mine and a sustained price fall for major exports. Official reserves declined steadily to a half-month of nonmineral imports in 1993, on account of large nonmineral sector deficits and substantial capital outflows. Strong mineral sector exports and the introduction of a floating exchange rate helped to correct the situation. The sharp contraction in key commodity exports in connection with the 1997 drought and the Asian financial crisis again gave rise to a large external current account deficit and another financial crisis in 1999.

Economic Recovery after 2000

To rein in financial imbalances, the government that took office in mid-1999 embarked on a reform program. The effort was aimed at stabilizing the economy and fostering private-sector-led growth through structural reforms. As a result, the budget deficit was substantially reduced, and the external current account surplus widened, reflecting large depreciations of the kina. However, the budget deficit rose sharply in the run-up to the 2002 elections, reflecting large overruns in spending. Structural reform slowed in response to military opposition to public sector downsizing and violent student demonstrations.

Macroeconomic performance has improved since the formation of the present coalition government in 2002. The government embarked on a comprehensive medium-term development strategy aimed at promoting private-sector-led growth and alleviating poverty. Economic stabilization and recovery started to take firm hold in 2003, after three years of negative growth, and there has been positive economic growth since, in response to improving performance of the agricultural and mining sectors. Meanwhile, inflation dropped sharply from a peak of 20 percent in 2003 to about 1 percent in 2005, reflecting fiscal and monetary discipline as well as exchange rate appreciation. In response to declining inflation and a firm foreign exchange market, the central bank progressively eased monetary policy.

The budget was brought under control, reaching a surplus by 2004. The turnaround largely reflected the sharp decline in domestic interest rates, higher mineral revenue, higher grants from Australia, and lower-than-budgeted development outlays. The government used most of the budget savings to reduce the stock of domestic arrears and to retire debt, although the civil service wage bill remained high. The improved fiscal outcome resulted in a reduction in total public sector debt to about 50 percent of GDP.

Overall, the country's external position has strengthened considerably in the recent past. While the economy stagnated in 2000, the current account surplus widened. The current account deteriorated again in 2002, because of large declines in mineral export volumes. Yet surpluses were restored in 2003 and beyond, underpinned by a sharp rise in export volumes together with buoyant international prices and lower nonmining imports. External official reserves rose to historically high levels by 2005.

Exchange Rate Management

Following about two decades of a fixed exchange rate regime after independence, Papua New Guinea switched to a managed float regime in 1994. In the early post-independence years, the government considered that a stable or appreciating exchange rate was crucial for reducing uncertainty related to mining activities and for controlling inflation. In addition, the country's strong balance of payments position, the result of buoyant mineral exports, alleviated competitiveness concerns. The kina was pegged to the Australian dollar during 1975–78. When the kina's parity came under stress in 1978, the government pegged to a trade-weighted basket of currencies of the country's main trading partners.

During the 1980s, Papua New Guinea retained the fixed exchange rate regime, but step devaluations were implemented in response to severe shocks. The weakening of export prices in the early 1980s, as well as the closure of the Bougainville copper mine and higher prices for oil and other imports, increasingly called for a downward adjustment of the kina to diversify nonmineral exports and increase employment. As a result, the government devalued the kina against the basket by 10 percent in 1983 to strengthen the country's competitiveness.

The government shifted to a floating exchange rate regime in 1994, to alleviate the pressures on the kina and restore external balance. The expansionary fiscal stance launched in 1992 had triggered high inflation and led to a marked deterioration in the balance of payments. In addition, regulations on capital flows were eased, leading to capital outflows and the near depletion of international reserves. In response, the kina was again devalued by 12 percent in 1994. The kina depreciated further in the aftermath of the adoption of the floating exchange rate regime by some 35 percent in nominal effective terms in 1995. With fiscal restraint and improved balance of payments outcome in 1996 and most of 1997, the exchange rate remained broadly stable on a nominal effective basis. From late 1997 to 1999, however, the kina depreciated continuously, but in recent years this trend has been reversed.

The floating exchange rate regime has served the country well in its efforts to absorb major shocks. The fiscal slippages ahead of the 2002 elections were met with a substantial depreciation of the kina. The restoration of macroeconomic stability since then, through fiscal restraint and prudent monetary policy, as well as much higher commodity prices, has led to steady appreciation of the kina and record official reserves.

Structural Policies

Implementation of the structural reform agenda remains largely unfinished. Reforms in several areas are crucial for achieving private-sector-based, medium-term economic sustainability. These include reforms that address shortcomings in the efficiency and governance of the public sector and state enterprises, promote public development spending and private investment, amend land tenure, and improve the law-and-order situation.

Central bank independence was established by legislation in 2000. The central bank is required to publish semiannual reports outlining monetary policy developments and prospects. Beginning in 2005, the monetary framework was expanded to a three-year horizon, from the previous six-month horizon. The central bank's supervisory role has been considerably expanded and now covers a wide range of financial institutions, including the four commercial banks (two of which are branches of major Australian banks), finance companies, superannuation funds, savings and loan societies, and life insurance companies.

Legislation in 2000 set the framework for enhanced financial system soundness, when licensing and supervision of banks and nonbank financial institutions were strengthened in line with best international practice. The banking system was reshaped in the wake of the privatization in 2002 of the country's largest commercial bank, with about 40 percent of total bank assets, which was sold to a private domestic bank. The soundness of the banking system has improved in the aftermath of the privatization, as evidenced by the improvement of key prudential ratios. Specifically, the share of nonperforming loans to total loans has been reduced, and asset quality and liquidity ratios have improved markedly, to well above prudential requirements. These favorable developments reflect continued improvement in credit procedures, strengthening of corporate governance, and strict application of fit and proper criteria for commercial banks' board members and senior managers.

The solvency of the two largest superannuation funds has been restored in the wake of reforms launched in 2000, when a major crisis affected the viability of these two funds—the National Provident Fund for private sector employees and the Public Officers Superannuation Fund for public employees. The crisis emerged as a result of large losses, unsound investments, and deficient corporate governance. The 2000 Superannuation Act paved the way for improved management and supervision of the funds, with the central bank designated as the supervisory agency, and both funds have experienced a financial recovery.

External trade arrangements have been progressively liberalized. The tariff reform that began in 1996, with reductions in rates on selected duties and the elimination of import bans on selected items, was stepped up in 1999 with the launching of a seven-year tariff program. The latter aimed at establishing four major ad valorem tariff rates (zero, 30, 40, and 55 percent) by 2006 and lowered the average nominal tariff on imports. Papua New Guinea has ratified PICTA and PACER.

Policy Challenges Ahead

The present government's development objectives for 2005–10 are set out in the Medium-Term Development Strategy. It is based on establishing good governance; promoting export-driven, nonmineral sector growth, especially in agriculture, forestry, fisheries, and tourism; and accelerating rural development and poverty reduction. These goals are to be met through public sector reform; an improved environment for private sector business; and a redirection of public investment toward rural infrastructure, basic education, and primary health care programs, including HIV/AIDS prevention.

The financing of the strategy is mapped out in a medium-term framework that accompanies annual budgets. The overarching goal is to foster macroeconomic stability while achieving stronger sustainable growth and poverty alleviation objectives. Although economic prospects under the scenario are generally more favorable than in the 1990s, they critically hinge on continued fiscal consolidation in tandem with prudent monetary policies and steadfast structural reform.

Real GDP growth is expected to pick up toward the end of the decade, as a gas pipeline project to Australia and the Ramu nickel mine come on stream. Growth in nonmineral activity would be led by buoyant agricultural output. Inflation is expected to be contained, assuming continued fiscal restraint and monetary discipline in concert with a broadly stable kina and moderate wage increases. The external current account would go into deficit, reflecting large goods and services inflows associated with the gas and nickel mine projects, but would improve toward the end of the decade as these are completed.

Achieving these development objectives depends crucially on continued fiscal consolidation. The government's medium-term fiscal strategy focuses on securing savings in wages and lower-priority budgetary spending while shifting resources toward infrastructure, rural development, health, and education. The government aims to maintain budget balance, with both revenue and expenditure declining steadily as a percentage of GDP. The anticipated revenue decline as a share of GDP primarily results from the contraction in mineral revenue in response to the ongoing depletion of established mines and oil fields and the expected softening in mineral and petroleum prices. In addition, the phasing out of the mining levy and completion of the tariff reduction program in 2006 will contribute to further erosion of the revenue base. The success of the fiscal strategy will depend on downsizing the civil service payroll, streamlining unproductive development projects, and strengthening budget management.

Reducing Papua New Guinea's debt is a core objective of the medium-term strategy. Despite reductions since 2002, total public debt outstanding remains at 50 percent of GDP (Figure 13.3). Under the present strategy, public debt would be reduced to a more sustainable level through 2010,

Figure 13.3. Papua New Guinea: Public Debt
(In percent of GDP)

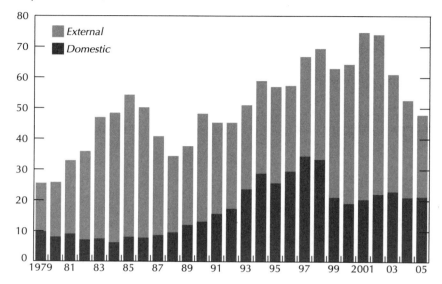

Source: National authorities.

through fiscal consolidation, improved growth prospects, and a gradual restructuring of the government's debt portfolio. The risks associated with the domestic public debt portfolio are expected to be minimized by switching from short-term treasury bills to longer-term inscribed stock and by curtailing the most costly nonconcessional external debt. As a result, the debt-to-GDP ratio is expected to decline to about 41 percent by 2010. Meanwhile, external debt is expected to decline as a share of total public debt during 2005–10. The downside risk to external debt sustainability would stem primarily from exogenous shocks, and the economy would be particularly vulnerable to exchange rate shocks.

14

Samoa

LAMIN LEIGH

Samoa consists of nine islands in the South Pacific, the two largest of which are Upolu, where the capital, Apia, is located, and Savai'i, which has a total land area of 2.8 square kilometers. Samoa has a narrowly based economy and, like many of the Pacific island countries, is highly vulnerable to weather-related shocks. It is heavily dependent on private remittances, which are equivalent to about 25 percent of GDP, to finance consumption and on official transfers to finance investment. Expatriates tend to maintain very strong ties with their families, villages, and churches, and this is true even among second-generation migrants. Emigration, which is primarily to Australia, New Zealand, and the United States, has kept the population stable at roughly 180,000 over the past decade. The political system is based on a parliamentary system of democracy and is stable.

Economic Developments since Independence

Inconsistent policies from the mid-1970s to the early 1990s made Samoa one of the weakest performers among the Pacific island economies. In the first decade after independence in 1962, conservative financial policies ensured the preservation of budget balance. However, there were subsequent episodes of macroeconomic imbalances and prolonged periods of stagnation. Expansionary expenditure policies were implemented in an attempt to accelerate growth, but these found little success and resulted in severe balance of payments difficulties and increased inflation.

These developments prompted a major review of economic policy and the introduction of a comprehensive economic reform program in 1996. Since then, Samoa has implemented wide-ranging structural changes, which have been supported by sound macroeconomic policies. In fact, Samoa is the most successful example of reform in the region. The authorities' biennial Statement of Economic Strategy has provided the overall macroeconomic framework for stability and structural reform, and there are separate strategies that focus on health, education, and rural development. Strong and stable political leadership, close consultation with stakeholders, and extensive efforts to foster a broad consensus for reform have been integral to the program's success. The major challenge now is for Samoa to press on with the reforms, especially to improve the conditions for private sector development.

Weak Performance during the 1970s, 1980s, and Early 1990s

During the second half of the 1970s, a series of IMF-supported economic adjustment programs were adopted to correct domestic and external imbalances. However, domestic financial policies did not support external adjustment, and the programs generally fell short of their objectives. With a lack of buoyancy in budget revenue and strong growth in expenditure, including wages and salaries, public sector deficits were large and these were financed by the banking system. Monetary policy instruments were unable to constrain demand for imports; balance of payments pressures were fended off only by tight exchange controls. The tala exchange rate was depreciated, on a trade-weighted basis, by 25 percent in 1975 and 19 percent in 1979. This contributed to rising domestic prices for imports, but there was no improvement in competitiveness because the depreciations were not supported by demand management policies.

As a result, other Pacific island economies performed better than Samoa during this period. Most of the newly independent island countries enjoyed sound external positions, which reflected buoyant export markets, plentiful concessional assistance, and cautious demand management policies. Deteriorating terms of trade in the early 1980s caused a pronounced weakening in external current accounts across the region, but most countries made the required external adjustment through a progressive tightening of fiscal, monetary, and wage policies. For Samoa, by contrast, the failure to implement appropriate policies contributed to a sizable fall in relative income, high rates of inflation, and severe external financing problems.

The economic decline was finally reversed during 1983–85 through firm implementation of comprehensive adjustment policies, supported by two IMF Stand-By Arrangements. The central government budget moved from deficit to surplus by 1985. Revenue increased sharply, reflecting both tax policy measures and improved tax collection. Spending was constrained by curbs on the growth of public sector employment, wages, and salaries; postponement of lower-priority projects; and an improved system of expenditure control. A strong recovery in international commodity prices and depreciation of the tala, on a trade-weighted basis, by 18 percent in 1983, strengthened the external position, and there were current account surpluses for the first time in more than 10 years. Sound demand management policies consolidated these gains over the following several years, although the growth rate remained disappointing.

The economy was again thrown off course during the first half of the 1990s by a number of major shocks. These included two cyclones, which devastated infrastructure and coconut and copra production; a blight that destroyed taro, the primary agricultural crop; and a financial crisis at the publicly owned airline. The result was a substantial decline in output and foreign reserves and an increase in public debt to over 90 percent of GDP. Economic recession in Samoa's major trading partners lowered exports, tourism, and remittances. Cyclone rehabilitation entailed a large increase in public investment, leading to overall government budget deficits in 1992–95.

Economic Transformation during 1996–2005

Samoa embarked on a remarkable economic transformation in the mid-1990s. With sound macroeconomic and strong reform policies, the economy outperformed comparator countries both within and outside the region (Figure 14.1). There was solid growth and low inflation, public finances and international reserve levels improved, and the level of public debt steadily declined.

Fiscal Policy

The fiscal measures included in the program of macroeconomic stabilization and reforms launched in the mid-1990s included steady cuts in expenditures and several tax measures, most notably a 10 percent value-added tax on goods and services (VAGST) and lower tax incentives. After a decade of fiscal prudence, the public debt ratio now stands at roughly 50 percent of GDP, almost all of which is external and is contracted with official creditors on concessional terms, especially to the

Figure 14.1. Samoa: Real GDP per Capita
(Index 1990=100)

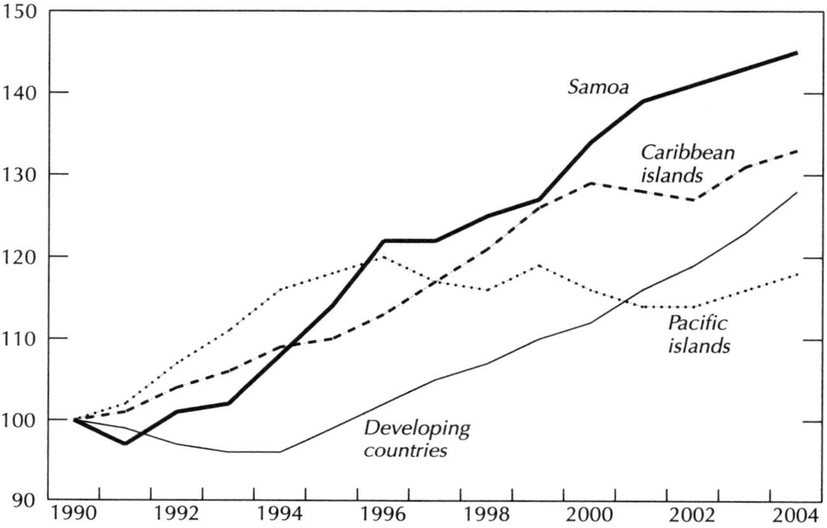

Source: IMF, World Economic Outlook database.

Asian Development Bank (ADB) and the World Bank's International Development Association (IDA). Debt service represents only 6 percent of exports of goods and services. However, because Samoa is exposed to various shocks, including natural disasters, the debt position can undergo rapid and large swings, and the government plans to lower the debt ratio further.

The fiscal measures taken in the mid-1990s and strong growth through 2001 helped contain the overall deficit below 2 percent of GDP (Figure 14.2). However, growth started to slow after 2002, and the government took several measures to limit the impact on the budget, notably on the revenue side. The VAGST rate was increased to 12.5 percent, and excise taxes were raised on a range of products, including alcoholic beverages, petroleum products, and tobacco products. As a result, the overall deficit has been brought down to less than 1 percent of GDP.

The level of revenue to GDP has been increasing (Figure 14.3). Total revenue, excluding grants, is at 22½ percent, very close to the average for other tourism-based island economies. Although revenue from import duties has declined continuously over the past few years, this has been more than offset by the VAGST and excise taxes, which now represent

Figure 14.2. Samoa: Evolution of Samoa's Budget Deficit
(In percent of GDP)

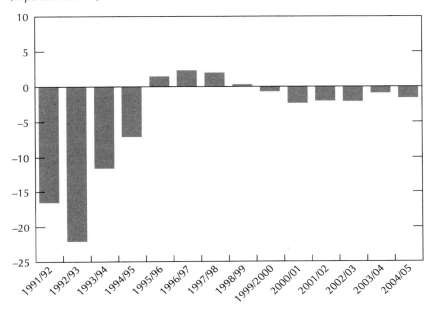

Sources: Samoa authorities and IMF staff calculations.

one-third and one-sixth of tax revenues, respectively. Indirect taxation, largely dependent on consumption, represents the bulk of tax revenues. As a result, the sensitivity of revenues to GDP downturns has diminished.

While the level of fiscal expenditures is broadly in line with other Pacific island countries, its composition differs. Samoa spends a larger share of its budget on capital expenditure and public investment projects, which are largely financed by foreign donors. In contrast, spending on the public sector wage bill is below that of comparator countries in the region. At the same time, Samoa does not have a well-developed social safety net. There has been steady progress in reforming the civil service. The restructuring exercise undertaken in 2003 reduced the number of government ministries from 28 to 13, plus four Constitutional Agencies. There have been 12 Institutional Strengthening Projects focused on improving the efficiency and effectiveness of government operations. There was a large downsizing of the Ministry of Public Works in 2001, with subsequent reductions in staffing levels relying primarily on natural attrition and a general freeze on funding for vacant posts.

Figure 14.3. Samoa: Total Revenue and Tax Revenues
(In percent of GDP)

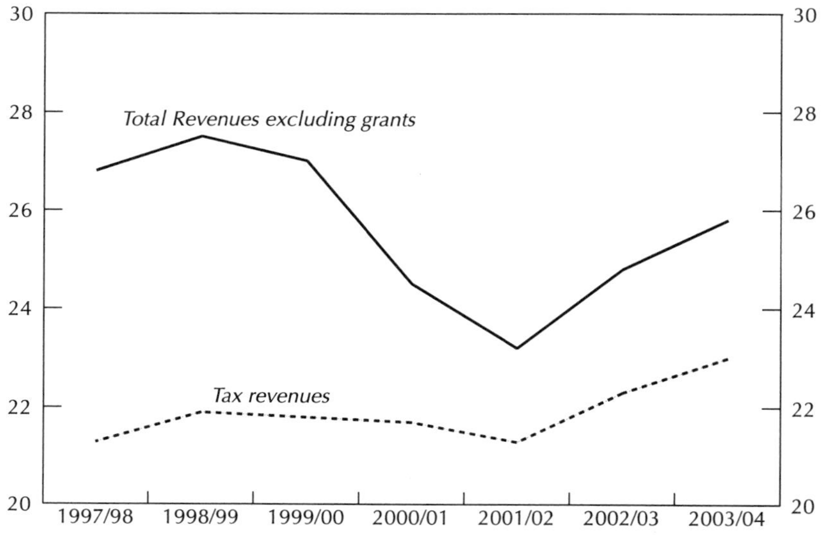

Sources: Samoa authorities and IMF staff calculations.

The Public Service Commission is leading a review of all existing ministries, with a view to refocusing them on their core functions. Implementation of the legislative framework underpinning financial management reforms is not yet complete. The Public Financial Management Act of 2001 did not officially come into force until 2003. After that, the subordinate regulations and finance instructions underpinning the act took considerable time to prepare. In addition, the Companies Act of 2001, which was designed to strengthen the operations of state-owned enterprises and make them more commercially oriented, was delayed by the need to incorporate bankruptcy and litigation provisions.

Weaknesses in fiscal transparency were highlighted by the Financial Management Improvement Project 2003–08 Implementation Plan, which emphasizes the need for improved budget documentation and more timely fiscal reporting. These proposals will be implemented on a phased basis, beginning with a financial management information system. Next will be development of a more timely and comprehensive budget formulation process, including medium-term budget forecast estimates and, later, better monthly and quarterly financial reporting.

Efforts are being made to strengthen the governance and account-ability of state-owned enterprises, in line with the Public Bodies Act, which provides the policy framework. A first step was to establish a monitoring unit and to launch institution-strengthening projects in Samoa Telecommunications, the Electric Power Corporation, and the Samoa Water Authority. All enterprises are now required to submit annual corporate plans to the Ministry of Finance. Divestment of minority share-holdings in Computer Services Limited, National Pacific Insurance, and Samoa Breweries is under way, and the Agricultural Store, Samoa Shipping Services, and Samoa Broadcasting Corporation are to be privatized.

The state-owned Polynesian Airlines has been a persistent burden to the budget. During the second half of the 1990s, the government cut much-needed spending on education and health to keep the airline operating. Subsidies averaged 3 percent of GDP annually during 2001–04. In addition, the government took over the airline's debt and provided guarantees for bank debt and aircraft leases. Polynesian Airlines was restructured as a joint venture with an Australian partner in 2005 and is expected to become profitable in coming years.

Monetary and Exchange Rate Management

Before the 1996 structural reforms, direct controls on interest rates and credit had inhibited financial sector competition and monetary policy implementation in Samoa. The controls resulted in artificially low deposit interest rates, which contracted savings, and rigid loan rates, which precluded risk-based credit pricing. Combined with volatile inflation, this caused wide fluctuations in real deposit and lending rates, constraining the level and efficiency of financial sector activity. In addition, supervision was weak, with only limited supervisory capacity at the central bank and no effective supervision of nonbank financial institutions.

Financial sector liberalization and the introduction of indirect monetary policy instruments were a major part of the 1996 structural reform program. All credit ceilings and interest rate controls were removed in 1998. Auctions of central bank bills began and became the primary monetary policy instrument. In addition, the liquid asset requirement was reduced and eventually abolished in 1999. These changes had a positive impact on financial institutions and markets. Credit to the private sector grew more rapidly, and banks' profitability improved. Programs were launched to strengthen the central bank's capacity to undertake prudential supervision, including for nonbank financial institutions and insurance companies. These liberalization measures facilitated faster real GDP growth during 1999–2003. Credit growth, in combination with sales of central bank bills, substantially reduced excess liquidity in the banking system. The Central Bank of Samoa then eased monetary policy in order to support economic activity following the 2004 cyclone.

Monetary policy is conducted in the context of a pegged exchange rate arrangement supported by capital controls, with the tala linked to a basket of currencies based on transaction-weighted trade, remittances, and tourism receipts. This regime has served well as a nominal anchor. The central bank periodically makes adjustments in the value of the tala within a plus or minus 2 percent band in order to strike a balance between maintaining external competitiveness and preserving the exchange rate peg's role as an anchor for inflation.

Regional indicators, despite some recent appreciation, do not signal an overvaluation of the tala nor do they suggest any loss of competitiveness within the region. External current account surpluses were recorded during 1998–2004, and official reserves were adequate. Export growth has stalled over the last few years, but this was due not to a lack of competitiveness and/or movements in prices and costs out of line with Samoa's major trading partners, but rather to the effects of unfavorable weather on fishing, which remains the largest export industry. There are plans to build more efficient landing and docking facilities to assist the fishing industry, and there are efforts to shift toward new export crops, although improvements in the agricultural sector are likely to be gradual. New Zealand recently entered an agreement to enhance Samoa's market access for higher-value-added goods, including organic crops and processed food, and to help diversify the export base. The Samoa Tourism Development plan seeks to strengthen this sector, which is seen as a promising engine for growth and is underdeveloped compared to some Pacific islands. Tourism will get a boost if the recent Polynesian Airlines merger is successful in lowering the high airfares. Remittances are expected to remain substantial.

The Financial Sector

The financial sector remains sound, and progress has been made in strengthening the supervisory framework, as noted. The four commercial banks, two of which are subsidiaries of major Australian banks, have a joint market share of over 75 percent of total banking system assets, are adequately capitalized, and are in compliance with the 15 percent capital adequacy requirement. The central bank's current practice is to conduct examinations through external auditors and extensive off-site monitoring, along the lines of the New Zealand model, and this is effective. Information is shared among the central bank, the external auditors, and the foreign banks, whose parent institutions maintain strong internal controls on their subsidiaries, and this reduces the need for an extensive on-site monitoring.

Samoa continues to make progress in tightening the regulatory requirements for offshore banks and strengthening the framework for anti–money laundering and combating the financing of terrorism (AML/CFT). The international banking bill approved by parliament in 2005 requires all offshore banks to establish a physical presence in Samoa and established an International Financial Authority as the supervisory agency for the offshore banks. An AML/CFT bill also was passed in 2005.

The authorities are reviewing the role and investment guidelines of the National Provident Fund (NPF) and are strengthening its supervisory framework. Its assets are now skewed in favor of short-term loans to members and to various public sector projects, and these borrowers can access about 50 percent of their outstanding balances, using their balances as collateral, because of the lack of long-term investment opportunities in the private sector. Thus, the government in 2005 gave the NPF the authority to invest abroad about 1½ percent of GDP or about 7 percent of its total assets.

Structural Policies

The public sector still dominates the economy, accounting for about 40 percent of both GDP and total employment. The goal is to reduce this share and enhance the contribution of the private sector to stimulate growth. The policy framework focuses on incorporation for state enterprises of strategic public interest, including power, ports, and water, and privatization for state enterprises in nonstrategic sectors. The Public Bodies Act stipulates that all enterprises be run on strict commercial principles. There are plans to inject more competition into the telecommunications sector, supported by an appropriate regulatory framework.

The reform program has helped improve the business and investment climate, but there are constraints on private sector activity that need to be addressed. Poor infrastructure is a concern, although public investment has been increased for road construction, telecommunications, and port development. Approval procedures for new businesses (domestic or foreign-owned) remain lengthy, and a one-stop shop is to be established to alleviate these bottlenecks. Addressing such structural weaknesses is critical not only to stimulate domestic employment and growth but also to invigorate and diversify the export base.

Land reform is important for private sector development. Most of the sites suitable for commercial development are on communal land, but the constitution bars the sale of communal land for commercial purposes. The challenge is to build an institutional and legal framework capable of sustaining an efficient lease market, while safeguarding the interests of the local community and protecting investors.

Trade has been liberalized, and there has been progress toward accession to the World Trade Organization. Since 1998, the maximum tariff rate has been reduced from 60 percent to 20 percent, the tariff schedule has been simplified to four rates, and rates of 35–42 percent have been reduced in several steps to 8 percent. Samoa is a founding member of PICTA, which aims to eliminate all intraregional tariffs by 2011. Samoa is also a participant in the negotiations currently under way for new access to the EU market through reciprocal Economic Partnership Agreements, which are expected to take effect in 2008.

15

Solomon Islands

EDIMON GINTING AND NATHANIEL PORTER

Solomon Islands is a collection of islands in the South Pacific, with the second largest land area among Pacific island countries, after Papua New Guinea. The six main islands account for 80 percent of the total area. The population of about 470,000 has been increasing by about 3 percent annually for the past few decades, one of the fastest rates in the region. Over 90 percent of the residents are Melanesians, and about 80 percent live in small, dispersed rural settlements. The national capital area, Honiara, the only urban center, accounts for a smaller percentage of the total population than in other countries of the region. There has been very little migration to other countries since independence and remittances are therefore minimal.

The country was a British protectorate from 1893 until independence in 1978. Parliament, elected every four years, selects a prime minister who in turn appoints a cabinet. In the absence of strong party allegiances, governments have essentially been coalitions. Political consensus has often been difficult to achieve and sustain, and this has hampered the cohesive and timely implementation of economic policies, including the development of medium-term strategies. Moreover, the authorities have faced considerable pressure to devolve power to the provinces, and increasingly so after civil conflict erupted in mid-1999. This conflict had its roots in ethnic tensions that were exacerbated by uneven development and other sociopolitical issues and exacted a significant economic and political toll.

Solomon Islands has had a volatile economic history, with weak institutions, difficult fiscal management, and frequent external shocks.

Improvements in living standards occurred only during limited periods. The economic structure, which has changed little during the last three decades, is characterized by a large public sector, very modest growth in private sector activities, and exports dependent on timber and a few other primary commodities. Annual GDP per capita, at $550, is the lowest in the region and has declined by about one-quarter since 1999 because of the severely negative economic effects of the civil conflict.

The economy was stabilized, and recovery started after the arrival of the Regional Assistance Mission to the Solomon Islands (RAMSI) in 2003, an initiative to restore law and order that is led by Australia and involves contributions from a number of South Pacific governments and the deployment of civilian, police, and military personnel. However, the challenges facing Solomon Islands are enormous. The key requirement is to sustain growth and broaden its base, while safeguarding macroeconomic stability. To this end, it is essential to strengthen fiscal management, reduce aid dependence, and accelerate structural reform. In particular, logging needs to decline to sustainable levels, and this will require creation of an environment conducive to growth in other sectors.

Economic Developments since Independence

Growth and External Developments

Because the economy is very open, it has been greatly influenced by the impact of natural disasters, terms of trade shocks, and the availability of foreign assistance, as well as local political and social difficulties. These problems have been compounded by rapid population increase. Subsistence farming and fishing still account for at least one-third of production, and this provides some measure of resilience in periods of economic downturn. There is no social safety net in the country, but some support is provided by the Wantok system, a complex set of reciprocal obligations, including the sharing of income and property among tribal members. Despite sizable fluctuations in economic activity, inflation has generally remained moderate to low, moving largely in line with changes in import costs.

At the beginning of the 1970s, timber emerged as a principal export, and fishing was transformed from a subsistence occupation to a commercial activity through a joint venture between a Japanese fishing company and the government. Palm oil production was established through another joint venture with foreign investors. Increased export activities produced

Figure 15.1. Solomon Islands: Current Account Balance
(In percent of GDP)

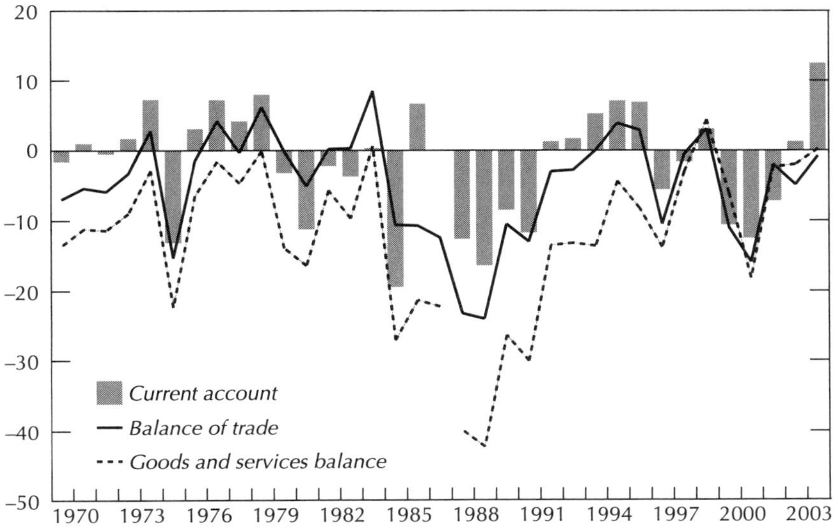

Source: IMF, World Economic Outlook database.

rapid economic growth (averaging almost 9 percent) in the second half of the 1970s and resulted in a sustained improvement in the external current account, which recorded surpluses amounting to as much as 6 percent of GDP. Combined with foreign direct investment and other capital inflows, the currency appreciated in both real and nominal effective terms and external reserves rose.

The vulnerability of the narrow economic base then became apparent. The 1980s was a turbulent decade (Figure 15.1), with several terms of trade shocks and a devastating cyclone. The prices of copra, palm oil, and timber all fell during 1980–83 which, together with the end of direct British budgetary support, resulted in current account deficits and low economic growth averaging less than 2 percent annually (Figure 15.2). A cyclone in 1986 caused extensive loss of life and damage to infrastructure and agricultural crops. The impact continued to affect exports for several years, resulting in lower incomes and imports. The recovery, which only commenced in 1988, was initially prompted by the acquisition of new fishing vessels and the opening of a fish cannery, but was broadened with improvements in the palm oil, copra, and logging sectors and with a cushioning of the balance of payments by increased grants. Nonetheless, in light of weak

Figure 15.2. Solomon Islands: Real GDP
(Index 1993=100)

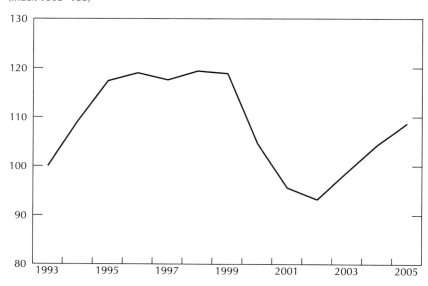

Sources: IMF, World Economic Outlook database; Solomon Islands authorities; and IMF staff estimates.

macroeconomic policies, this fell far short of preventing external reserves from falling to extremely low levels.

Solomon Islands' weak external position and natural disasters led the government to use IMF resources. There were two Stand-By Arrangements, the first in 1981 and the second in 1983. Less than half the amounts agreed under these arrangements was actually disbursed because the authorities were unable to fully meet conditionality requirements and did not request the last three purchases under the second program because the external position improved in 1984. The country also tapped the emergency assistance facility following the 1986 cyclone.

The first half of the 1990s saw a turnaround in living standards. Economic growth reached an average of 8 percent annually, inflation moderated, the external position strengthened, and the real exchange rate stabilized. Much of this improvement was driven by improved terms of trade, especially higher timber prices, which encouraged new entrants and quickly added to capacity. The increase in agricultural and timber exports brought about a marked reversal in the current account, to a surplus. Even a cyclone in 1993 slowed growth only temporarily. The improving trade and current accounts continued through the middle of the decade. This period masked the fundamental weaknesses resulting from the heavily concentrated economic base, high cost structure, and weak public finances.

The improvements of the first half of the 1990s were undone by these economic and institutional weaknesses and the Asian crisis. The logging boom abruptly ended with reduced Asian demand. This caused the economy to contract, despite investment in a gold mine and increased foreign aid. Depreciation of the currency did not arrest the deterioration in the external position because of the lack of supporting financial policies.

The economic decline worsened when long-running ethnic tensions erupted into civil conflict in 1999. Growth plummeted, the real economy shrank by one-third, infrastructure was destroyed, and the external current account deteriorated, as major foreign investment export projects closed. Notwithstanding a peace agreement in 2000, the conflict continued until the arrival in 2003 of RAMSI (Box 15.1). Until then, external reserves cover remained minimal, even though the central bank gradually depreciated the exchange rate against the U.S. dollar by over 30 percent during 2002.

The end of hostilities and the restoration of law and order brought economic recovery and stabilization. Real GDP growth averaged over 5 percent in 2003 and 2004. Inflation fell from its conflict peak of 16 percent to 8 percent in this period, partly as a result of exchange rate stabilization. The end of the ethnic violence also allowed a resumption of private sector activity, especially timber exports, and began to pave the way for the return of foreign investment projects. Much greater foreign assistance helped stimulate growth and an improvement in the external position, with the current account moving to a surplus of 12 percent of GDP in 2004 from a 7 percent deficit in 2002. Foreign reserves reached historically high levels.

Fiscal Developments

Solomon Islands has experienced repeated fiscal imbalances in the last three decades. The budget position weakened considerably immediately after independence in 1978. Current outlays increased rapidly, reflecting the transfer of functions to the newly independent government and enlargement of the administration. Capital outlays picked up quickly due to the expansion of inter-island transport, fishing fleets, and infrastructure projects. Deficits often emerged in subsequent years, because of difficulties in containing the wage bill and revenue erosion through extensive tax and

Box 15.1. Solomon Islands:
Ethnic Conflict and Foreign Intervention

The ethnic violence that intensified in mid-1999 had been developing for a long time. The indigenous majority on Guadalcanal harbored animosity against migrant workers from the island of Malaita, based on the perception that they enjoyed greater success in the competition for jobs and resources. Further, Malaitans gained control of a growing portion of land in Guadalcanal as a result of steady migration in recent decades.

In mid-1999, bands of armed militants from Guadalcanal intensified attacks on workers of Malaitan descent—many of whom were second-generation migrants. Malaitan militia groups were formed and launched retaliatory attacks. In early 2000, these groups united into the Malaita Eagle Force. For their part, the native Guadalcanal armed militias united into the Isatabu Freedom Fighters. Limited international assistance was insufficient to strengthen the government's control over the police and to improve its capacity to address the security threat.

Peace negotiations culminated in October 2000 with the signing by the government and the main parties of a peace agreement in Townsville, Australia. A cornerstone of the agreement was the government's decision to compensate the victims of ethnic violence. The payments were financed by a loan from Taiwan Province of China, but much of the loan went toward payments to the militants, who often secured their payments by force, at the expense of those who lost property.

The peace agreement did not fully achieve its chief goal of disarming the militants. Many guns were surrendered as part of the amnesty in the months after the agreement was signed, but most militants continue to be well armed. In return for signing the agreement, participating militant groups were awarded amnesty for most criminal acts committed during the ethnic violence, and this led to bitterness on the part of the victims. Random acts of violence continued in and around Honiara, often by ex-militants who had been absorbed into the police force.

Faced with continued economic decline and internal unrest, the government requested foreign assistance to restore law and order and stabilize the economy. An Australian-led intervention force of nine Pacific countries with over 2000 military and police officers arrived in mid-2003. The Regional Assistance Mission to the Solomon Islands (RAMSI) quickly halted the violence, without bloodshed. Australia and New Zealand also placed their nationals in the judiciary and major budget departments to help the stabilization effort. No date has yet been set for the withdrawal of the intervention force, which may well be several years away. In fact, RAMSI was strengthened to quell a flare-up of the conflict in late April 2006, which was sparked by controversy over the composition of the newly elected government.

Figure 15.3. Solomon Islands: Public Debt
(In percent of GDP)

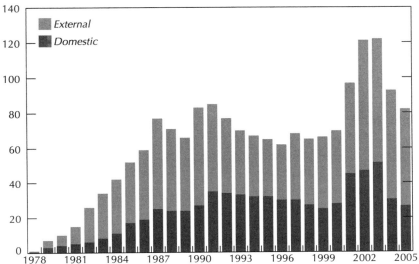

Source: Solomon Islands authorities.

customs exemptions. Throughout the period since independence, domestic revenue has been insufficient to cover current expenditure, and capital spending has been heavily dependent on external aid. Declines in grant disbursements generally led to cuts in public investment, but they also led on occasion to larger budget deficits.

The budget position remained weak during the 1980s. Current expenditure increased due to persistent expansion in the wage bill, higher transfers to local governments, and subsidies to cover the operating losses of public enterprises. To strengthen the fiscal situation, the government increased import duties and improved tax administration, although these policies were thwarted by inadequate expenditure controls. Despite the pickup in external grants after the 1986 cyclone, the budget deficit widened, owing to capital expenditure to finance cyclone reconstruction. The continued large deficits and depreciation of Solomon Islands dollar led to a large buildup of public debt, to 63 percent of GDP by 1989 (Figure 15.3).

Budget deficits also caused financial strain in the 1990s. After peaking at 13 percent of GDP in 1991, the deficit averaged 6 percent of GDP during 1992–97, largely due to revenue erosion through tax exemptions and declining grants. Initially, the deficits were financed by commercial banks and the National Provident Fund. Once these sources were exhausted, the government turned to the central bank, and by 1995 had exceeded its statutory limit on such borrowing. The government suspended interest payments to the holders of domestic securities in 1996, leading to the effective closure of the treasury bill market. With all sources of financing closed, the government incurred sizable domestic and external arrears.

In 1998, the government launched a program to strengthen public expenditure management. This helped bring the budget temporarily into surplus, owing in part to increased external grants to finance a reform package, reduce the number of civil servants, improve expenditure management and delivery of services, bolster tax collection, and reduce the scope and activities of the public enterprises. The budget position deteriorated again as revenue came under pressure after the decline of exports during the Asian crisis and civil strife. The government failed to restrain expenditure, and then made substantial payments to militants under the peace agreement. The deficit increased to 12 percent of GDP by 2001, largely financed by expenditure arrears and borrowing from the central bank. The government debt-to-GDP ratio rose sharply to 120 percent by 2002.

Fiscal mismanagement was turned around after the arrival of RAMSI in 2003. The government introduced a tax amnesty and strengthened tax administration. These efforts led to a sharp increase in the collection of all taxes, and the 2004 tax-to-GDP ratio jumped by nearly 5 percent of GDP compared to its pre-crisis level. The government ceased payments to ex-militants, carried out a payroll audit and eliminated ghost workers, and tightened expenditure controls. Donors' direct budget support and higher assistance for development spending helped stabilize the situation. With current expenditure below its pre-crisis level, a surplus of 8 percent of GDP was recorded in 2004. The restructuring of domestic debt and payment of some domestic expenditure arrears, together with strong growth, helped the debt-to-GDP ratio decline to 93 percent.

The 2004 surplus, however, was mainly due to temporary factors. Revenues included several one-time elements, including donor support and payment of back taxes, while logging tax receipts were based on an unsustainable rate of deforestation. On the expenditure side, capacity constraints caused underspending in improving education, health, and infrastructure. The 2005 budget registered a small deficit because of an increase in civil service wage rates and higher expenditure on basic service delivery and investment projects.

In 2004, domestic bonds held by the commercial banks and the National Provident Fund were restructured, and payments were made on other arrears. Bilateral donors repaid overdue credits to the World Bank and the Asian Development Bank. In 2005, the government, seeking to regularize its external arrears, started to negotiate with its creditors at a multilateral meeting, called the Honiara Club. Creditors agreed to some principles for debt relief, including a debt moratorium in the short term and a debt stock reduction at a later date, provided that the authorities adhered to some conditionality, including a policy of fiscal responsibility and progress in implementing the government's structural reform plan.

Exchange Rate and Monetary Management

The Solomon Islands dollar was introduced shortly before independence to replace the Australian dollar, which had circulated as domestic currency. The real effective exchange rate has remained broadly constant since the mid-1980s, although there have been substantial nominal depreciations to reflect inflation differentials. The first occurred during the 1980s because of terms of trade and natural shocks. The second followed the Asian crisis, when the exchange rate was depreciated by about 20 percent against the U.S. dollar. Third, during 2002 the rate was gradually depreciated by a cumulative 30 percent against the U.S. dollar to reflect the adverse effects on the balance of payments of the civil unrest. Since 2003, the central bank appropriately has kept the bilateral exchange rate vis-à-vis the U.S. dollar broadly constant rather than permitting an appreciation in the face of large inflows of external assistance, and this has allowed reserves to be rebuilt to a relatively comfortable level.

The central bank was established in 1983, and monetary policy in the 1980s and the 1990s attempted to achieve multiple objectives. In addition to maintaining price stability, the central bank aimed to reduce pressures on the balance of payments, meet government borrowing requirements, and support economic development by lending to state-owned and small-scale enterprises. It also directed credit to certain sectors through special refinancing facilities. From the mid-1980s, without the availability of indirect monetary instruments, the bank attempted to tighten liquidity requirements in the face of a weaker external position. However, the measures had only limited success due to the continued rapid expansion of credit to the public sector.

The banking system is performing satisfactorily. The troubled Development Bank of the Solomon Islands, which has large debts, is being liquidated, and depositors are being repaid by the central bank, the court-appointed manager. There are three commercial banks, two foreign banks with a combined market share of over 57 percent and a locally owned private bank. These are well capitalized and profitable, and their asset quality has improved with a decline in nonperforming loans in recent years. However, the financial position of the National Provident Fund is a concern, particularly because of its shareholdings in weak public enterprises, which were made in the past at government direction. Legislation has been adopted to address AML/CFT, and a financial intelligence unit is being established.

Structural Policies

The environment for private sector development has been weak throughout Solomon Islands' history. There is little tradition of commercial or entrepreneurial activity, and the Wantok system, which is prevalent throughout the country, often inhibits individual initiative. Moreover, there are considerable regulations and administrative procedures that hamper the creation and operation of businesses.

The legal regime governing foreign investment has been discretionary, with many activities reserved exclusively for Solomon Islanders, although a new law has been designed to address these problems. The difficulty of dispute resolution and other legal issues further inhibit the private sector. It can be difficult and costly to enforce contracts, with resolution often taking more than a year and costing more than the amount in dispute. The limited extent of private land tenure complicates the ability of businesses to open and obtain finance.

Infrastructure is generally lacking or in disrepair. Transportation infrastructure is poor. There are no roads in large parts of the country, and inter-island shipping, the most important transportation method, is unreliable. Private sector shipping has either been explicitly prohibited on some routes by provincial governments or made unprofitable by competition from subsidized provincial shipping lines. The state-owned airline has incurred losses, and inconsistent service has inhibited regional growth and tourism development.

Policy Challenges Ahead

Despite the economic recovery that has occurred since the end of civil disturbances, Solomon Islands faces enormous challenges to address long-standing structural problems. The critical need is to sustain the growth seen over the past couple of years, broaden the base of private sector activity, and address poverty, while maintaining sound fiscal and monetary policies. A major issue that must be addressed is that logging has been exploited well beyond its sustainable level, and its economic contribution must decline or forests could be exhausted by 2015. Palm oil production is expected to recommence in 2006, and gold exports are expected to resume in 2007, provided the security situation remains stable. It is critical to foster new private sector activities that can contribute to growth, including in agriculture, small manufacturing, and tourism.

16

Tonga

RAJU SINGH

Tonga is a small agriculture-based economy in the South Pacific with a population of about 100,000 and per capita income of about US$1,600. It shares a number of common characteristics with other Pacific island countries, including remoteness, openness, limited production diversification, and vulnerability to natural disasters, including severe cyclones in 1982 and 1991. The population size has remained broadly constant in recent decades, despite a high birthrate, because of large-scale emigration, mainly to Australia, New Zealand, and the United States. As a result, Tonga is a recipient of one of the highest levels of remittances in terms of GDP among all developing countries. These substantial inflows, coupled with the family-oriented, closely knit, traditional nature of the society, help to alleviate the poverty and social problems associated with the lack of employment opportunities. Health and education indicators are in line with or above the regional average.

Tonga is the only constitutional monarchy in the region. Although not formally independent until 1970, it maintained a greater degree of independence than most Pacific territories while under foreign rule. The kingdom, unified in 1845, was relatively isolated until becoming a British protectorate in 1900. Subsequently, the United Kingdom managed external relations, but its involvement in domestic affairs was limited. While the constitutional monarchy is based on the British model, the king exercises wide influence, including appointing the cabinet, which is led by the prime minister. The unicameral Legislative Assembly, which is elected every three years, consists of nine nobles chosen from among the 33 peers

Table 16.1. Tonga: External Indicators

(In percent of GDP)

	1980–90	1991–2000	2000–04
Trade balance	–44.0	–31.4	–33.3
of which			
Exports, f.o.b.	9.9	8.7	9.5
Imports, f.o.b.	53.9	40.2	42.8
Net private transfers	26.3	21.7	35.9

Source: Tonga authorities.

who are the traditional owners of most land; nine publicly elected representatives; and the cabinet ministers. Members of the royal family hold key positions in the public and private sectors, including telecommunications, electric power, banking, and retail trade.

Economic Developments since Independence

Growth and External Developments

Agriculture, forestry, and fisheries are the largest contributors to GDP, dominated by a limited number of products, including squash and tuna, which are vulnerable to exogenous shocks. Most of the rest of GDP is generated in services, including support for the public sector. The manufacturing sector is marginal. The balance of payments is characterized by large trade deficits, with exports representing about 10 percent of GDP and imports averaging about 40 percent. Although private remittances have increased markedly since 1970, Tonga also remains dependent on sizable levels of official external assistance.

The 1970s were characterized by relatively favorable macroeconomic conditions. The economy experienced some diversification, and public investment expanded. Real GDP growth averaged 3–4 percent annually. The balance of payments was sound, and generally registered an overall surplus. The external trade deficit, which resulted from a combination of stagnant exports and increased imports, was offset by tourist receipts, remittances, and external aid (Table 16.1). Official international reserves rose to comfortable levels.

During the 1980s and early 1990s, the economic situation deteriorated. Real GDP growth slowed to about 2 percent annually, as Tonga's main traditional exports, bananas and copra, declined and eventually disappeared in the face of low world prices and shipping problems (Figure 16.1).

Figure 16.1. Tonga: Real GDP
(1993=100)

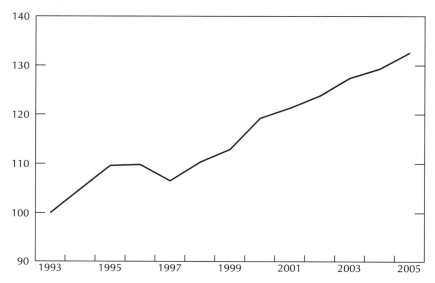

Source: IMF, World Economic Outlook database; Tonga authorities; and IMF staff estimates.

Another factor was the considerable reduction in Australian and New Zealand tariffs, which eroded the advantage to Tonga of its duty-free access to these markets. The introduction of squash production in the mid-1980s to supply Japan introduced some temporary dynamism and boosted agricultural incomes, but production peaked in 1993 and has since been in decline, partly reflecting growing foreign competition in that export market. Furthermore, even though squash production provided a welcome expansion of Tonga's export base, it meant the economy was dependent on a single crop. In response, the government adopted a strategy of promoting manufacturing, establishing an industrial park, and providing generous tax concessions. While the initial outcome was encouraging, production for the domestic market leveled off and exports dropped as tax holidays expired and tariff preferences continued to erode. Nevertheless, buoyant remittances and official assistance financed an increasing share of imports, and foreign reserves remained high.

Since the mid-1990s, economic performance has been mixed, with continued modest real GDP growth. A combination of policy slippages, governance and transparency problems, and weakened budget discipline have undermined macroeconomic stability and external viability. There has been persistent pressure on the budget, including from the large wage bill and ambitious public investment projects, and this has made it difficult to maintain fiscal control.

Problems were exacerbated by losses in the U.S. stock market and elsewhere that wiped out the Tonga Trust Fund, which had been established in 1989. By 2001, poor management and risky investments by the king's financial advisor had depleted the fund, which had amounted to about 20 percent of GDP in 1999. This further restricted the economy's ability to buffer adverse external shocks. With limited monetary policy instruments, the authorities relied primarily on increased exchange rate flexibility to protect official reserves, fueling double-digit inflation.

Fiscal Developments

Fiscal policy was conservative during the 1970s and early 1980s, but discipline weakened subsequently. There was an implicit rule requiring a recurrent fiscal balance, and this was relatively easy to observe initially because there was little need for domestic financing: capital expenditure was financed with concessional assistance, and public enterprises did not require budgetary subsidies. The government even built up considerable net deposits with the banking system. Fiscal developments deteriorated after the mid-1980s. With inadequate expenditure controls, current spending increased rapidly, including through sizable civil servant wage adjustments. Several large-scale public investments were financed with external commercial borrowing. In addition, the performance of public enterprises weakened, and budgetary subsidies grew. Notwithstanding measures to raise domestic revenue and continued external grants, overall budget deficits emerged that needed domestic financing.

Beginning in the mid-1990s, the authorities scaled back the size of the public sector, in response to the deteriorating fiscal position. Some government commercial activities were privatized and export monopolies were ended. Public finances were brought broadly back into balance by limiting the recourse to domestic financing through cuts in current and domestically financed capital spending and a freeze on civil service salaries. This improvement was, however, short lived. In the early 2000s, there were significant wage adjustments, and public enterprises required increasingly larger budget transfers and lending. Recourse to domestic financing intensified, and government debt reached about 60 percent of GDP in 2004.

The prospects for the medium term are highly uncertain. The civil service wage increase decided in September 2005 could create considerable difficulties for the maintenance of macroeconomic stability. Following a lengthy strike, civil servants were granted average wage increases of about 70 percent, payable over the next two years. The direct fiscal impact of this wage agreement is very substantial, possibly 8 percent of GDP, with potentially adverse inflationary and balance of payments consequences. In response, the government is seeking comprehensive offsetting measures and reviewing its fiscal strategy more generally.

Monetary and Exchange Rate Developments

With limited instruments, the authorities have little scope to anchor monetary growth. There are no clearly established target rates for monetary expansion, no means of ensuring price stability, and no medium-term policy framework. Movements in foreign exchange reserves are taken as an indicator of the appropriateness of monetary policy. The government considers that a relatively high level of reserves is desirable because of the fluctuations that characterize export receipts, the country's dependence on private and official transfers, and its distance from major commercial centers and transportation routes.

Monetary policy was largely accommodative prior to the establishment in 1989 of a central bank, the National Reserve Bank of Tonga. Monetary policy was carried out by the Treasury, other departments in the government, and the Bank of Tonga, created in 1974 to offer a full range of commercial banking services as well as to undertake certain central banking functions. The authorities exercised little control over the activities of the bank, including its credit operations, until 1982, when guidelines were instituted to safeguard the balance of payments, requiring that the bank limit new lending when foreign exchange reserves declined to below four months of imports. These guidelines were operational only for a short period of time, as the external position remained sufficiently strong and demand for credit was moderate.

The central bank itself was not much more successful in anchoring money growth and controlling credit expansion. During the 1990s, the bank conducted open-market-type operations to absorb liquidity by issuing its own notes, but it stopped issuing these notes in 2001 because of poor profitability and the resulting deterioration in its capital base. The bank has since resorted to credit ceilings and moral suasion to conduct monetary policy. The central bank continues to lack sufficient independence to pursue the requisite monetary operations, because its establishing act allows it to provide direct credit to the government.

During the 1970s and 1980s, Tonga's currency, the pa'anga, was pegged at par to the Australian dollar, even though the main source of imports was New Zealand. In periods when the pa'anga depreciated against the New Zealand dollar, inflation accelerated. In 1991, the authorities introduced a basket peg that included the U.S., Australian, and New Zealand dollars, and later the Japanese yen, to better reflect Tonga's trading patterns and developments in competitor countries. As the macroeconomic environment deteriorated during the 1990s, the peg could not prevent a real appreciation of the currency and an erosion of foreign reserves. Following the Asian crisis, the authorities decided to introduce greater flexibility in the arrangement by allowing the value of the currency to be adjusted in either direction by up to 2 percent per month if needed, and the pa'anga depreciated. The margin was widened to 5 percent in 2000 and used to depreciate the currency further to protect foreign reserves and preserve competitiveness through 2003. The central bank thereafter reversed its policy, as the level of reserves strengthened and concerns about inflation increased. Overall, the current arrangement has proved sufficiently flexible to protect the county's level of foreign exchange reserves in light of its vulnerability to natural disasters and terms of trade fluctuations.

Structural Policies

Private sector activity is small, as in other Pacific island countries, although in terms of business regulation, the country is not badly positioned. Available indicators show that Tonga compares favorably to other countries in the region in terms of labor market flexibility, contract enforcement, and the costs of starting and closing businesses (Table 16.2). However, the lack of transparency in the scope and implementation of regulations, including a discriminatory licensing regime, is identified by domestic and foreign investors as the most serious impediment to private sector development.

Land tenure issues also inhibit private sector growth. All land is ultimately owned by the crown, although in practice ownership is divided among the nobles, paramount chiefs, and government. In exchange for annual payments in cash or goods, every male adult is entitled to an allocation of several acres of land for his family's use, which may be transferred to male offspring and certain other relatives but cannot be sold. Leasing has been permitted under certain conditions since 1976, partly because land resources are no longer adequate to permit allocations to all eligible males. However, the traditional land policy prohibiting its sale and allowing only relatively short leases hampers long-term investment.

Table 16.2. Tonga: "Doing Business" Indicators

	Tonga	Selected Pacific Countries	East Asia and Pacific Countries
Labor market flexibility (index 0–100)[1]	7.0	15.1	24.0
Corporate disclosure (index 0–7)[2]	1.0	1.3	2.6
Contract enforcement (days)[3]	305.0	315.6	316.0
Starting business (days)	39.0	41.3	51.0
Closing business (years)[4]	2.7	3.0	3.4

Source: World Bank, Doing Business database.
[1]Higher index indicates more rigidity.
[2]Higher index indicates more disclosure.
[3]Measures the time of dispute resolution.
[4]Measures the time of bankruptcy resolution.

Public enterprises, which cover a wide array of activities from transportation to manufacturing, further constrain private sector development. In 2001, the government adopted legislation regulating the use of public resources by public enterprises, which requires trading activities to be operated along commercial lines and social and economic services to be separately identified. Progress in implementation has been modest. More recently, however, the government decided to liquidate the national airline, which has been a major source of financial difficulty since it expanded to provide international services in 1992, owing to poor management and unrealistic goals. Its liquidation is an important effort to contain the budgetary impact of poor performance.

Indicators of banking soundness are broadly satisfactory. The commercial banks, all three of which are foreign-owned, have strengthened their capital base, asset quality, and profitability in recent years. The Tonga Development Bank, majority-owned by the government, is being more closely monitored; its lending policies caused financial problems in earlier years. In the area of bank supervision, the Financial Institution Act has recently been amended to make the licensing and supervision of financial institutions consistent with Basel Core Principles. A Money Laundering and Proceeds Crime Act was enacted in 2000, establishing a framework consistent with international AML/CFT best practices and Financial Action Task Force on Money Laundering (FATF) recommendations.

Policies Challenges Ahead

Tonga's economy has become more vulnerable in many respects over the past three decades. The country's exports have not become diversified, and macroeconomic management has become more challenging. Tonga has managed, however, to weather adverse events to a great extent through emigration, which has provided a solution to the lack of employment opportunities, and large inflows of remittances, which have helped to prop up domestic incomes and consumption. These favorable accommodations cannot be taken for granted in the future, underscoring the need for reform.

To lessen its dependence on remittances, Tonga needs to make its economy more dynamic. The country needs to diversify its production and export base. Agriculture, fishing, and tourism are the best sources for future economic growth. Developing these sectors will require promoting the private sector. Tonga is a small economy, remote from its main export markets, and without a large pool of entrepreneurs. Even so, it can reduce a number of current obstacles to the development of the private sector, including by ensuring a stable macroeconomic environment through fiscal consolidation and improved monetary management. The main medium-term policy objective is to raise the rate of sustainable economic growth and alleviate poverty.

With regard to budgetary issues, the most difficult task will be to achieve a sustainable fiscal adjustment over the medium term. In the past, public finances have periodically been brought back into balance through expenditure compression. These adjustments have been achieved mostly by cutting operations, maintenance, and domestically financed capital expenditure and by freezing public sector salaries, neither of which can be sustained indefinitely. Future fiscal adjustment will need to focus on achieving a sustainable reduction in the wage bill. The public sector remains large and needs to be downsized and rationalized around the core functions of the government, by means of a hiring freeze, outsourcing of public services, and early retirement packages, for which external support for severance payments might be available.

The authorities also should proceed with tax reforms to reduce Tonga's heavy reliance on import duties and the excessive tax burden on some sectors. With further trade liberalization under way, other revenue sources need to be increased. A broad-based, single-rate consumption tax for large businesses has recently been introduced. The corporate and personal income taxes still need to be simplified and a more uniform customs duty rate adopted. In addition, extensive tax incentives should be repealed and replaced where necessary with accelerated depreciation and investment allowances. At the same time, in view of its revenue impact, reforms must be accompanied by intensified efforts to improve tax and customs administration.

With regard to monetary policy, greater use of indirect monetary instruments is vital to control aggregate demand. A framework based on open-market-type operations is needed to maintain monetary control. This is now even more crucial, as the 2005 public sector wage increase could create additional inflationary and balance of payments pressures. Although in recent years the central bank's profitability and capital position have improved, future open-market-type operations should use treasury bills, rather than central bank notes, to avoid undermining the bank's financial situation. To further strengthen the financial autonomy and independence of the bank, legislative amendments should be passed to increase its capital and to strictly limit direct central bank credit to the government.

Finally, structural improvements in the business environment are crucial for increasing investment, productivity, employment, and growth. These should include a simplified regulatory regime for investors and clarification of the boundaries between the public and private sectors so as to level the playing field. The legal framework for securing property rights should be strengthened and the land tenure system amended to extend the duration of leases. Such changes could elicit a much-needed boost from private investors.

17

Vanuatu

SUSAN CREANE

Vanuatu is an archipelago of 80 islands in the South Pacific. Like similar economies in the region, Vanuatu's economic growth was modest in the decade following independence in 1980. Average growth was somewhat faster in the 1990s, but it faltered in the early 2000s (Figure 17.1). The country fulfills many of the theoretical requisites for faster growth. It has a relatively sound macroeconomic environment, with low public debt, limited inflation, and an open trade regime. It has substantial natural resources and undeveloped fertile land. It is closer than most other Pacific islands to prospective markets for tourism in Australia and New Zealand. Finally, the relative homogeneity of the population of 215,000 (the third largest in the Pacific) shields the country from both ethnic disruptions and problems associated with crime.

Despite its advantages, Vanuatu continues to provide a weak environment for private activity, with poor infrastructure, rapid population growth, and political instability, and this has compounded the difficulties stemming from the still narrow output and export base. Human development indicators, including literacy levels, are among the lowest in the region. About 40 percent of the population is below the poverty line, and 80 percent of the labor force is employed in subsistence activities in rural areas. While annual real GDP growth has averaged about 3 percent since independence, relatively rapid population growth has resulted in little increase in per capita terms. Achieving a level of economic growth that can lift living standards significantly will require greater structural reform.

Figure 17.1. Vanuatu: Real GDP per Capita
(1990=100)

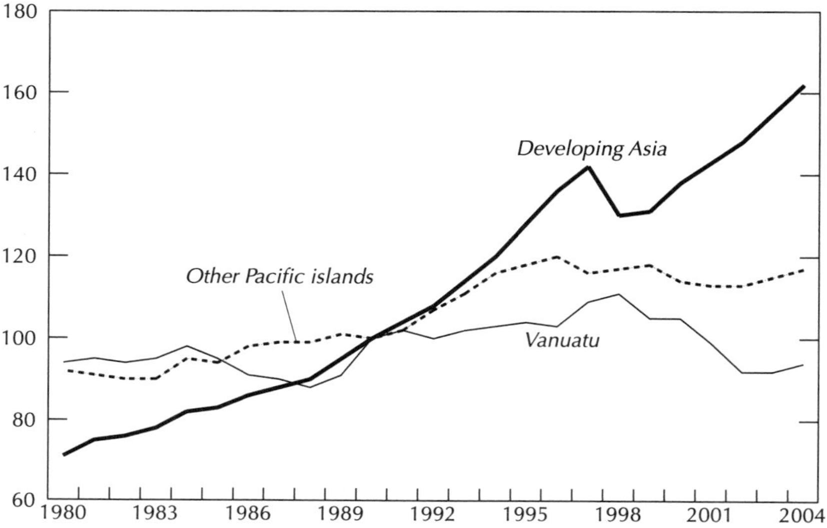

Source: IMF, World Economic Outlook database.

A diffused political system has made it difficult so far to introduce the reforms needed to encourage private sector growth. Prior to independence, Vanuatu (then New Hebrides) was governed jointly by France and the United Kingdom. Two political parties dominated politics under the Anglo-French condominium, one identified with Anglophone voters and one identified with Francophone voters. At independence in 1980, these two parties splintered into more than 10 political parties plus independents. No party regularly earns a majority of the vote of the 52 parliamentary seats. The resulting coalition governments have often survived only for short periods, because political unions are frequently created and dissolved.

Improving Vanuatu's growth performance will require, in addition to political stability, increasing investment in human capital and infrastructure, redirecting government expenditure toward development spending, and improving the environment for private investment. Private sector development is constrained by the lack of available financing, poor transportation and communication infrastructure, land tenure disputes, high business costs, and opaque investment rules.

Economic Developments since Independence

Economic Structure

The country is well endowed with natural resources, including abundant and fertile land, sufficient rainfall to support a wide variety of crops, and waters rich in fish. About 70 percent of export goods are cash crops, mainly copra, coconut oil, cocoa, beef, timber, and kava. The narrow export base has left earnings highly sensitive to changes in world prices, weather, and demand. The natural tourist attractions include unspoiled beaches, reefs, and active volcanoes. Tourism is the most important source of foreign exchange, at double the size of goods exports.

The industrial base is small and limited to light manufacturing, such as processed foods. A desire to expand the production base and a related search for a niche in services led to establishment of Vanuatu's status as a tax haven (no income, estate, or death taxes are levied) and development of an offshore financial sector. The country also offers flag-of-convenience registration of ships. The monetized sector of the economy is concentrated in the two main urban areas, and subsistence agriculture remains the principal livelihood for about 80 percent of the population.

Imports are relatively high, as a result of the limited production base and a large expatriate population. Consumer prices are largely determined by import prices, which in turn are significantly influenced by prices in the main trading partner countries (particularly Australia) and by the exchange rate of the vatu.

The importance of services has been rising since independence—in particular, tourism and the offshore financial sector. Since the early 1990s, the services sector has driven overall real GDP growth. The importance of the public sector has declined, although it remains large, and there continue to be large state enterprises. The trade regime remains open. Vanuatu has relatively low levels of tariffs and nontariff barriers and participates in the regional trade initiatives, PICTA and PACER. The banking system is relatively large and, although considered sound, it is exposed to a number of potential risks related in part to its dual nature (domestic and offshore). Total deposits are more than double GDP, because of the offshore banks. Financial sector oversight has been strengthened considerably in recent years, especially for offshore banks. The number of offshore banks was sharply reduced in 2003, and the remaining banks were brought under the Reserve Bank of Vanuatu's direct supervision and made subject to standard regulations, such as the requirement of a physical presence. The domestic market is served by three commercial banks (two foreign). The nonbank off-

Table 17.1. Vanuatu: Consumer Prices
(Average annual change)

	1980–89	1990–99	2000–05
Vanuatu	9.0	3.3	2.4
Pacific Islands	8.2	5.9	5.8

Source: IMF, World Economic Outlook database.

shore financial sector has been subject to an increased level of supervision. There is a pegged exchange rate regime, with the vatu linked to the French franc until 1981 and then to the SDR. The current adjustable peg, adopted in 1988, is linked to a transaction-weighted basket of currencies.

Economic Performance, 1980–90

In its first decade, Vanuatu's economic performance was uneven. There were setbacks to real GDP growth related to independence, including the departure of skilled expatriates, a decline in tourist arrivals, and a rebellion on the outer islands. After a recovery in 1981–83, the economy was hit by a number of cyclones in 1985–88, which caused significant loss of life and crop damage. In addition, in 1986 one foreign air carrier discontinued service to Vanuatu, which reduced the number of tourists. Consumer price inflation closely tracked exchange rate developments throughout the decade and averaged about 9 percent (Table 17.1).

The fiscal position deteriorated as the authorities faced a decline in foreign assistance while grappling with the large inherited public sector. Foreign grants fell sharply, from 80 percent of government expenditure in 1980, to 50 percent in 1983, and 21 percent in 1989 (Figure 17.2). A unitary government was introduced after independence, but it was impossible to fully streamline all the government functions undertaken by the condominium's three separate administrations (French, British, and domestic) and to integrate the dual systems for education and other public services. The government struggled to meet its commitment to minimize deficit financing by taking steps to tighten expenditure and increase revenue, mainly through fees, charges, and import duties.

Public expenditure increased with post-cyclone reconstruction during 1995–98. Domestic revenue only partially offset the combination of increased expenditures and declining foreign grants, and overall government balances moved from a surplus of 6 percent of GDP in 1984 to a deficit of 9 percent of GDP by 1989. The government began to incur new external debt, in part to finance the Development Bank of Vanuatu, although most

Figure 17.2. Vanuatu: Fiscal Balances and Debt
(In percent of GDP)

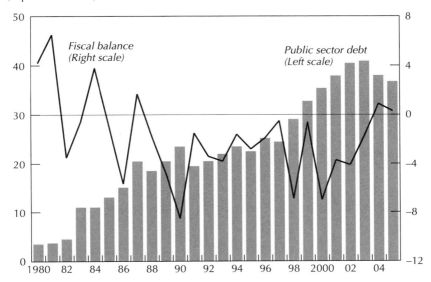

Source: IMF, World Economic Outlook database; and IMF staff estimates.

such debt was on highly concessional terms. Together with the domestic borrowing required to cover fiscal deficits, government debt increased to about 17 percent of GDP by the end of the decade, compared with about 3 percent of GDP inherited from the condominium government.

The external accounts generally stayed in surplus because receipts from tourism offset small net outflows on the capital account. Performance was poor immediately after independence, but it improved when expatriates and tourists returned as the political situation improved. However, external conditions worsened at mid-decade because of the cyclone damage, declining commodity export prices, and reduced air service. In addition, a downturn in the Australian economy and depreciation of the Australian dollar contributed to a fall in tourist arrivals. By the end of the decade, the vatu had depreciated by 26 percent, including a revaluation by 5.6 percent in 1984 and cumulative discrete devaluations in 1985–86 that totalled 29 percent.

The Reserve Bank of Vanuatu was created in 1980, but with few resources to carry out its mandate. One of its first tasks was the successful exchange of New Hebrides franc notes and other circulating currencies with the new vatu notes. During the 1980s, the bank also experimented with direct controls, in particular ceilings on loan rates, in order to encourage investment.

In response, banks acted to protect their margins by imposing additional charges while keeping deposit rates unchanged. The result was high effective interest rates on loans and, given the highly open economy and rapidly growing offshore sector, outflows of capital seeking higher returns. By the end of the decade, administrative controls were removed, and interest rates were determined by the market and were positive in real terms.

Improved Performance in the 1990s

During the 1990s, Vanuatu experienced growth rates on a par with comparable countries in the region. Rapid expansion of the services sector was strong enough to offset the uneven performance of agriculture, which suffered weather-inflicted damage. Construction was boosted by the implementation of large foreign assistance projects, including an international telecommunications network and the airport runway extension. The latter improved tourism receipts by allowing larger aircraft to service international passengers. Business in the offshore center also continued to increase. At the same time, inflation moderated as the vatu appreciated against the main import and trading partners (although depreciating overall on a nominal effective exchange rate basis). The appreciation was partly a result of a number of measures taken by the government (including lower import tariffs and the elimination of trade monopolies). As noted, political instability and weakening governance had a negative impact on economic activity, including by delaying necessary reform and influencing investor confidence. A Comprehensive Reform Program was launched in 1998 with the objective of improving economic and financial management and strengthening institutions to facilitate faster growth.

The fiscal accounts continued to be weak, despite periodic efforts at consolidation. Large supplementary appropriations were made in several years, including upward adjustments to the wage bill, notwithstanding the civil service reform objectives. New taxes, including a turnover tax, and fees did not offset net reductions in import duties, resulting in an overall decline in tax revenue. At the same time, discretionary import duty exemptions and weak enforcement led to substantial revenue losses. Development expenditure remained high, but foreign borrowing and weak oversight of the process for selecting projects led to a continued buildup in debt, which almost doubled to 33 percent of GDP by 1999.

The Reserve Bank sought to strengthen its capacity for monetary management and bank supervision, in particular by introducing indirect instruments, including central bank bills. During this period, the exchange rate peg of the vatu usefully provided a nominal anchor for domestic prices and fostered confidence in the financial community. However, in the absence of effective supervision of the domestic and offshore banking sector, loan quality problems emerged at the state-owned National Bank of Vanuatu and the Development Bank.

Falter and Recovery: 2000–05

Economic growth was modest during 1999–2002. The immediate causes were the cyclone damage to the agriculture and tourism sectors and the weak external environment, although the underlying causes were the persistent structural weaknesses. Progress on the Comprehensive Reform Program had waned by 2000, owing to a lack of consensus about the appropriate policy direction.

The Vanuatu economy has recovered since 2003, with real GDP growth rebounding to 3 percent annually in 2003–05. The recovery was bolstered by strong exports, even in the face of further cyclone damage. There was a recovery in export prices for key crops, an increase in tourist arrivals with an expansion in airline capacity, and liberalization of trading in cacao and copra. The pegged exchange rate regime helped keep inflation subdued, and the vatu remained broadly stable in real terms. The external current account deficit narrowed with the stronger performance in tourism and exports.

There has been considerable fiscal consolidation since 2000, from a deficit of 7 percent of GDP to a small surplus of about 1 percent of GDP in 2004–05. However, this is due in considerable part to compressed spending on social services and infrastructure, which could hamper medium-term growth. The wage bill is still more than half of total expenditure, which is large by regional and global standards. The delivery of basic services to the outer islands continues to be poor. Total public debt fell below the government's limit of 40 percent of GDP in 2004, but will be difficult to keep on a downward trend.

The financial sector has been strengthened significantly during the last few years. The Reserve Bank's supervisory regime was extended successfully to the offshore sector. A financial intelligence unit was established, and AML/CFT legislation amended as needed. Plans are under way to improve the supervisory oversight of the nonbank financial sector.

Policy Challenges Ahead

Deeper reform will be required to improve growth over the medium term. Without an active reform effort that addresses infrastructure weaknesses and other factors that raise the cost of doing business, real GDP growth could remain at the current moderate level, which would mean only modest gains in per capita GDP, given the high population growth rates. Pressures to raise current spending could also bring a return to fiscal deficits. With a stronger reform effort, growth could rise to allow a faster improvement in per capita GDP over the medium term. The reforms should focus on reorienting fiscal spending to well-targeted social and infrastructure needs. The targets for increased infrastructure spending are roads, electricity, water, and transportation in both the main and outer islands. Given its narrow base, the economy will remain vulnerable over the medium term, and its resilience will depend on the extent of structural reform. It will be important to preserve political stability and maintain good relations with major donors. Indeed, recent improvements in the political and economic situation have been reflected in an increase in donor assistance from Australia and New Zealand and in Vanuatu's qualification for the U.S. Millennium Challenge Account. These inflows will fund infrastructure investment over the next five years.

The government's long-term fiscal objective is to run surpluses in order to allow for debt repayment and contingencies such as natural disasters, and to increase development expenditure in order to achieve a higher level of sustainable economic growth. However, development expenditure is still declining and is among the lowest in the region, and so there is a considerable distance to cover before this strategy can be realized. The realignment of expenditure must include lowering the public wage bill, which is high by regional and global standards, and reforming public entities that are either partially or entirely government-owned and receive direct budget grants. In addition, there should be limits put on discretionary tax and duty exemptions to public and private enterprises, which are relatively large. The structural weaknesses that constrain private sector development should be addressed. This will involve increasing investment in human capital and infrastructure and redirecting government expenditure toward development spending. It will also require improving the climate for private investment by expanding the availability of financing, improving transportation and communication, resolving land tenure disputes, reducing the high costs of doing business, and making investment rules more transparent.